TILTING

AT

RELIGION

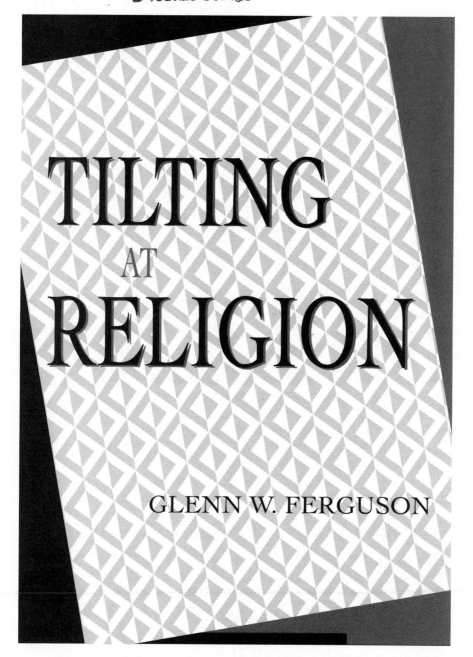

TILTING
AT
RELIGION

GLENN W. FERGUSON

 **Prometheus Books**

59 John Glenn Drive
Amherst, New York 14228-2197

Published 2003 by Prometheus Books

* Before each major section, an original aphorism by the author is incorporated. If one of the author's aphorisms from a previous book appears: *Unconventional Wisdom—A Primer of Provocative Aphorisms* (Tempe: Pen Art Productions, 1999), it will be followed by an asterisk.

** A few original essays found in this book appeared in a previous book by the author: *Americana against the Grain—A Collection of Essays* (Tempe: Pen Art Productions, 1999). A double asterisk will identify those essays.

Inquiries should be addressed to
Prometheus Books
59 John Glenn Drive
Amherst, New York 14228–2197

716–691–0133 (x207). FAX: 716–564–2711.
WWW.PROMETHEUSBOOKS.COM

07 06 05 04 03   5 4 3 2 1
Library of Congress Cataloging-in-Publication Data

Ferguson, Glenn W.
    Tilting at religion / Glenn Ferguson.
        p. cm.
    ISBN 1–59102–041–7 (alk. paper)
    1. Free thought. I. Title.

BL2747.5 .F47 2003
200—dc21   2002036619

Printed in the United States of America on acid-free paper

CONTENTS

10. RELIGION AND SOCIETY

11. EDUCATION AND RELIGION

12. DEMOCRACY AND RELIGION

13. PSEUDORELIGION

14. FUNERALS

15. CEMETERIES

16. CHURCH ESTHETICS

PREFACE

For a score of years, I have maintained a daily journal that incorporates my opinions and prejudices about American society, the world in which we live, and the varied professional interests I have discharged. Each essay in my journal is short, concise, and direct.

In 1999, a book of satirical essays and a book of creative aphorisms were published. It is now my intent to prepare tracts emphasizing specific subjects.

Most of the drafts of the essays that deal with religious practices, beliefs, and events were extracted from my journal. In addition, I have written several religiously oriented essays that are independent of the journal. Occasionally, they are based upon religious events I attended or churches I visited.

In the United States, in spite of the church-state separation doctrine, religion and society are interwoven. In most other countries, the interrelationships are even more profound.

Although most contemporary mores are predominantly social in origin, a significant number are based upon religious components. Even though most of us do not embrace a specific faith, we are confronted every day with the social impact of religious influence. In spite of these interrelationships, the Christian movement has only enhanced the prestige of the church, winning limited numbers of converts rather than improving the general welfare or the moral fiber of the bulk of humankind.

Religious partisans invade my world repeatedly and without sanction. In return, it is my belief that I should be encouraged to submit critical judgments about their world. My motive is not to disparage religious beliefs, but to attack the untrammeled certitude of unthinking, insensitive religious zealots of all faiths. Unfortunately, when a religious thesis is not subject to proof, we tend to endorse or ignore the trumpeter who believes while deprecating the nonbeliever.

Believers often accuse nonbelievers of many infractions and indiscretions that have been devised by the believers to discourage others from nonbelief.

An atheist is a person who rejects the existence of a supreme being, specifically God. In the late sixteenth century, the concept was created by religious devotees with vested interests.

An agnostic is a person who believes that, in the absence of evidence, it is impossible to ascertain whether there is a God. This term was not devised until 1869. Agnostics also believe that the "ultimate cause" is unknown. By using the existing religious concept of God, rather than relying upon his/her neutral intellectual powers to investigate the unknown, the agnostic begs the question.

To compound a felony, the accusation of blasphemy is invoked. At the beginning of the thirteenth century, it was devised by representatives of the organized church. It is seldom recognized that blasphemy was initiated by the Greeks and Romans several centuries before the birth of Christ.

For the past seven hundred years, the organized church has sought a refuge from rationality by alleging that those who do not share the visions of the church, and express their opinions, are guilty of blasphemy and should be subject to the imposition of sanctions.

Blasphemy can be defined as an irreverent, profane, impious utterance or act of behavior pertaining to God or anything considered sacred. With that generic definition, it is difficult for a writer to play according to the other guy's rules. I have attempted to approach the task with respect for all beliefs and disapproval of religious jingoists who are engaged in imposing their beliefs on others.

There are a few nuggets of hope. A recent federal court ruling states that witchcraft is a legal religion, and even the Dalai Lama has overtly admitted that he does not possess supernatural powers.

It is my belief that the majority of thinking Americans, a generous percentage of whom are nonbelievers, are cowed into silence about religion because of overt and veiled threats from those discharging religious power. Without aspiring to offend the sensitivity of any reader, I am hopeful that this book of essays will facilitate a more meaningful dialogue.

BELIEFS

1

Christianity was created by endorsing a myth.

THE CREDO OF THE IGNORED

I do not believe in God. I do not believe in any person's definition of God. I object to the assumption that the unknown, which is becoming more complex, must always be characterized as "God." I do not believe in miracles, in the Holy Ghost, or in any ghosts; in the Immaculate Conception; in organized religion; in the ritual of any church, or in the substance or resulting life style of any religious dogma.

I believe in the potential of humanity. I will continue to strive for the improvement of human beings. I believe in government, even more government. I believe that the rich should pay higher taxes; that welfare programs should be reintroduced with improved management; that public service should be nurtured, and that service, in any form related to the public weal, except religious service, should be generously rewarded by society as well as by the Internal Revenue Service.

I believe that private enterprise should be encouraged; that corporate takeovers should be controlled; that business ethics should be enforced. In my view, compensation for businesspeople should be related to comparative standards that reflect the objectives of a more enlightened society; that teachers should be paid more than professional athletes; that merchants should be treated like hucksters; that the stock market should be subject to rigid supervision; that free trade should be encouraged; that a balanced budget should be implemented, and that public servants should be compensated realistically.

I believe that capital punishment should not be imposed, even for egregious crimes; that those who sell hard drugs should be subject to life sentences; that abortion should be sanctioned, and that citizens who refuse to exercise restraint regarding the size of the family should be sterilized.

I believe that English should be the language of instruction in the public schools (and should be the principal language in the halls of government), and that every high school graduate must complete a minimum of two years in a language other than English or the language that is spoken primarily in the home.

I believe that realtors should be monitored; that the sale of environmentally sensitive land should be subject to a prepurchase review; that the environment should be protected in support of a viable national policy; that automobiles should be excluded from downtown metropolitan areas, and that handguns should only be licensed when significant external violence threatens national security.

I believe that the United States must maintain its military strength; that full detente with Russia and China (subject to civil rights enforcement policy) should be approved; that the partially civilized nations should declare war on terrorism; that Israel should be treated as a foreign country; that Japan and Germany should pay fully for their own defense; and that the United States should not export military weapons. The lesser-developed world should receive increased assistance from the wealthy nations (if birth control practices are enforced); Americans should not be granted passports to serve as missionaries abroad; the military draft should be reinstituted, and the Peace Corps and Americorps should be considered alternate service (to military duty). The federal government should increase its support of higher education; two-year colleges should become terminal technical programs; educational television and radio should be readily available, without commercials, in every home; and lawyers should be deported to Liberia.

This credo could be extended. The conclusion is obvious. I am a liberal, internationalist, and a fiscal conservative who endorses humanity (assuming that the number of our species is gradually reduced), recognizes little of value in anything related to organized religion, and I am convinced that contemporary American society is headed in the wrong direction.

The majority might inquire: "Why don't you go live in Denmark?" I am an American. I am proud of my country's achievements and potential. In Denmark, I would be considered a foreigner (even more than in the United States). Of greater importance, it is only in the United States (and in a few other countries) where a person with the beliefs I have described can be guaranteed the fruits of freedom.

I am dedicated to the proposition that the United States could become an exemplary country in which to live and work. Based on the political eras of Presidents Nixon, Reagan, Clinton, and Bush II, it has become a second-class country in terms of basic values. I am also confident that this society is nurturing an increasing number of people who share many of my beliefs. Our present numbers can be easily ignored by the majority.

Childhood Exposure to the Church

As a youngster in Syracuse, New York, I attended Sunday School at the Erwin Methodist Church on Euclid Avenue. My father was raised a Baptist in Virginia and my mother as a Methodist in the same state. After leaving Virginia as young adults, neither of my parents attended church regularly.

My mother was convinced that I needed exposure to formal religious instruction. To honor her wishes, I complied. At the age of ten, every Sunday morning, I walked more than a mile from our home to church. The other young participants did not attend my public grade school. I never attended the regular Sunday church service, only Sunday School.

I learned a few prayers, memorized the Beatitudes, and absorbed a list of readings from the Bible. For almost two years, I compiled a perfect attendance record. At the age of twelve, when I joined the Boy Scouts, I informed my mother that I would no longer attend Sunday School. In later years, my mother became an active Christian Scientist.

I have been introduced to several religious faiths: I attended summer services at the Church of Jesus Christ of Latter-day Saints in

American Fork, Utah, and participated in miscellaneous denominational church services in the United States and overseas. I was baptized and married in the Episcopal Church.

In retrospect, I am reassured that my mother requested that I become indoctrinated in organized religion. Early in life, my introduction to the Erwin Methodist Church allowed me to make a partially educated judgment about the relevance of the organized church in my life.

BELIEF AND REALITY

A belief not subject to proof should not impinge upon reality. I can believe in democracy and work for its perfection. In time, either I or my successors will be able to evaluate the results of my efforts. If democracy, in the context in which I am involved, can be improved, it is possible to judge whether the approach and the program have had positive impact.

If I believe that God only blesses those who are left-handed or those who abstain from birth-control practices, my beliefs are not subject to proof. When I contribute to a church that facilitates my identification with the heaven-bound proclivities of left-handed people, I am engaging in innocuous behavior. I may feel better, and my spare cash will probably not be allocated for drugs or for one-armed bandits. If the church that disdains right-handers develops a program in Africa to keep right-handers out of the school system, my belief becomes serious. When a church states that God does not want an impoverished African to use a condom, somebody gets hurt.

In a democracy we cannot proscribe charitable idiocy or forbid devotees of unprovable religious beliefs from choosing up sides. At the same time, there should be a minimal effort to make certain that our concept of the unknown does not create roadblocks for those in Africa, or elsewhere, who have never been exposed to a particular version of the gospel.

The person (elected) who resides in the White House must inform the religious believers in the electorate that their private religious approach to birth control dogma must not dictate the foreign policy of the United States. It is patently clear that many countries require birth control and planned parenthood programs. Independent of the abortion issues, which represent a substantive difference of opinion, the national leadership must risk the alienation of a few believers in order to insure the health and survival of many people at home and abroad. Beliefs should not be controlled, but beliefs that cannot be proven, and that ignore the manifest realities of the world in which we live, must be eschewed in formulating realistic public policy.

To allege that the world is round does not represent an article of faith. To allege that God tells us that the world is round does represent an article of faith. To allege that God wants us to reject planned parenting in Africa and Asia does represent an article of faith and should not become the cornerstone of the failure to act. Religious belief and reality must be distinguished. As usual, I am baying at the wind, but as a believer might say, "what's a heaven for?"

POWER AND RELIGIOUS BELIEF

Religious proclivities are seasonal, cyclical, and unpredictable. Conventional wisdom assumes that agnosticism, atheism, and religious disinterest are products of the twentieth century. In fact, during the French Revolution, atheism was more prevalent than at any other time in Christian history.

Identification with organized religion is a function of the relationship between secular and religious power. If those in power (in all walks of life) endorse or patronize religious dogma, or the absence thereof, religious sentiments will be nurtured or inhibited accordingly. If those in power actually oppose organized religion, or a specific body of religious thought, and they add sanctions to that opposition, they are not playing by the rules of the game and must be eschewed.

Most of us tend to believe, and certainly to practice, what we are told to believe by those who hold power, interpret power, or feed on power. Left to our own intellectual devices, few of us would have convictions about God or those who interpret God. Religious belief represents choice, and unless we are told that we cannot believe or disbelieve, there is little pressure for involvement. If everybody else were atheists, and insisted that I repudiate organized religion, I would probably believe in God.

ARE BELIEFS SUBJECT TO CHANGE?✷✷

I have been brooding about the difficulty of changing any person's belief about any subject. At some unknown point in childhood, a human being endorses a point of view. He or she becomes more or less liberal or conservative, a believer or a nonbeliever, right to life or free choice, straight or gay. As maturity intervenes, changing that belief or way of life becomes a formidable task.

With the possible exception of born-again fundamentalist religious conversions, generally captured on prime-time television, I am unaware of any comparable conversion of attitudes or ideas in the real world.

At a relatively early age, we accept or reject a point of view expressed by a parent, classmate, teacher, parson, or friend or incorporated in some form of communication. It is virtually impossible to document the time frame when the point of view or belief became our own, but once claimed, it is difficult to alter.

For pragmatic reasons, a politician may switch party affiliation, but I am unaware of any politician who was converted from a John Bircher to a United Nations advocate overnight.

When a belief is captured, experience that tends to refute that belief is ignored. Beliefs nurtured at an early age become impregnable barriers to education or even discussion.

Whenever I am informed that education is a partial answer to contemporary societal problems, I find my mind wandering. Conceivably, if the requisite educational miracle occurred early in life, beliefs could be subject to refinement or alteration. Unfortunately, I do not know which beliefs warrant inculcation, who should be responsible for inculcating them, or at what age or in what forum the process should occur. I am only aware that I have never been able to change the other guy's point of view and, by God, he will not change mine!

THE YEAR OF OUR LORD (ACCORDING TO DIONYSIUS)

In 1279 A.U.C. (*ab urbe condita*—"from the founding of Rome"), Dionysius Exiguus created the Christian chronology to settle a lengthy dispute regarding the proper method of calculating Easter. Dionysius was a Scythian (a tribe residing north of the Black Sea) monk who was also probably an abbot.

In that year, several chronological systems were utilized; however, none figured the years consecutively from a fixed starting point. In fact, it is doubtful that Dionysius used 1279 A.U.C. as a matter of course, but that he calculated the date in order to devise the Christian chronology. Existing Christian chronologies such as the "indication" (based on tax periods of fifteen years) and the "Era of the Passion" (used briefly in eleventh-century France) afforded only a short-term methodology for the chronology in years.

Dionysius discarded the Diolectian calendar (based on the Alexandrian era), which began in A.D. 284 because he did not want to honor the leader whom he considered a "great persecutor." Alternatively, he decided to base the annual chronology on the year in which Jesus Christ was born.

According to the Book of Matthew, Christ was allegedly born during the reign of Herod the Great. Since Herod died several years prior to the year selected by Dionysius for Christ's birth, his computation was vitiated by a minimum error of at least four to six years, assuming that the Matthew scripture was based on fact.

Since the date of the founding of Rome was problematic, and the date selected by Dionysius was suspect, the A.D.-B.C. Christian chronology is undoubtedly inaccurate. By custom, it is no longer subject to scrutiny.

Ignoring reality, Dionysius reckoned that Christ was born 754 years after the founding of the City of Rome. That year was designated A.D. 1. Subtracting the year that Christ was supposedly born from 1279 A.U.C. produced the year in which Dionysius created the Christian chronology as A.D. 525. Subsequently, it was ordained that there was no "zero" year between A.D. 1 and 1 B.C.; therefore, the years proceed from 1 B.C. to A.D. 1 without missing a beat.

Having solved the chronology issue with dispatch, Dionysius decided to begin each year on January 1. Previously, for a significant number of years, each year commenced on either December 25 or on Easter Day. The January 1 decision was not readily accepted. It is only during the last few centuries that January 1 has been definitively established as the beginning of each calendar year.

Until the seventh century A.D., the Christian chronology was ignored. During the eleventh century, it was used selectively in parts of Europe. Spain adopted the Christian chronology in the fourteenth century to insure that Columbus would discover America in A.D. 1492. The Greeks did not endorse the Christian chronology until the fifteenth century.

Other relevant chronologies also experienced difficult incubation periods. The Muslim chronology began July 16, A.D. 622, give or take a few years. The Buddhists and others devised systems that have gained acceptance. Since Esperanto has failed to generate acclaim as the universal language, it is unlikely that a standard chronology will warrant worldwide acceptance.

The Jews selected a remarkable starting point for their chronology: i.e., the year that Earth was created. Since that date has been moved back several billion years, through scientific experiment, it requires major leaps of faith to study history based on the Jewish chronology.

Now that the second millennium has arrived, there are a few minor problems concerning the year A.D. 2000. When A.D. 1000 rolled around, there were few folks who were aware of the Christian chronology. With the exception of a few fundamentalists who announced that the world would disappear when A.D. 2000 arrived, only a scattering of machines, and some humans who were born in a leap year, really took cognizance of the date.

If I decide to endorse the Gospel according to Matthew, I will be approximately six years older than I am at the moment. Given my advanced age, that calculation is totally unacceptable. Since the year A.D. 2000 is approximately 2754 years after the founding of Rome, I may switch to that chronology. Thus endeth the scripture.

THE DEITY

What did God do prior to the first day?*

IS THERE A GOD?

God was created by man to provide a possible explanation for the unknown. In recorded history established facts have not dissuaded the true believer who has merely created another God, or Gods, or redefined Gods, to explain the remaining elements of the unknown.

As we learn about our intricate universe, it is tempting to attribute the complexity to the works of God. However, either before or after the discovery of DNA, to endorse the existence of God is to endorse a fiction. Until that fiction is subjected to proof, members of any faith are precisely that, espousing a faith. All religious beliefs are figments of humankind's vivid imagination. "Miracles" occur because unexplained or contrived events transpire where factual precincts have not reported. To allege that the remaining mysteries can be attributable to God is increasingly suspect. Each new discovery based on scientific fact minimizes the chance that the remaining discoveries will corroborate the existence of God.

In an effort to refute this point, the true believer will ask "who made the first atom?" To demand the ultimate answer, as science gradually approaches that answer, is to ignore reality and to grasp for a religious straw. In the absence of any indication that a God exists, or that Gods exist, it is difficult to profess faith.

I am unhappy that equity does not always prevail in human relationships, and that human aggression inevitably leads to war; however, the limitations of some humans interacting with others does not point to the presence of God but to the inability of humankind to live in harmony. Aggression is related to chemistry, and limited education, and human frailty will not be corrected by heroin, faith in God, or any other escape from reality.

It hurts to realize that I will be castigated as a godless person by those who believe in God and by those (who may also believe) who lead less that exemplary lives. It is distressing to know that when I die, and when my progeny's progeny die, the existence of God will not yet be disproved. It is also devastating to recognize that formative young minds are turned away from science because of fear of the unknown. It is enervating to be aware that disparate beliefs in a fictitious God provoke wars, alienate neighbors, and provide a safe harbor for pirates masquerading as spiritual leaders.

If people with exemplary moral standards, better dispositions, or greater ability professed belief in God, I would consider taking the vow for pragmatic rather than for intellectual reasons. In the absence of a scrap of evidence that correlates faith in God with generic lives of distinction, I will remain a nonbeliever. If Earth were still considered flat, I would believe in God. There would not be any other explanation. An irrational universe would require an irrational belief in God.

"GOD, IF THERE IS A GOD"

"God, if there is a God" represents agnosticism. It would appear that the agnostic is perfectly willing to allow the God-fearing person to define the terms in a religious frame of reference.

"There is no God" represents atheism. It would appear that the atheist is perfectly willing to allow the God-fearing person to define a void as the manifestation of God and to use the word "God" in defining his lack of belief.

When a nonbeliever is attempting to search for life's meaning without acknowledging the prevailing concept of "god," he or she makes the task virtually impossible by spelling "God" or "Him" with a capital letter, by risking the charge of animism or blasphemy, or by failure to take the initiative.

Until we are able to discard the mystical and unsupportable tenets of every religion, it will be difficult to formulate a system of meaningful values that will sustain humankind to a terminal state called death.

Believers accept absurdities that have been devised by superior intellects and that create factions identified with intellectual niceties, none of which is subject to proof. There is no accountability for our actions except to ourselves, to a just or unjust law, or to a norm established by society.

A DEFINITION OF GOD

The illusory definitions of God, so vastly dissimilar that any two versions could not be true, have facilitated the creation of a multitude of sects and the perpetuation of organized religion.

To admit that the universe still contains mysteries does not lead to the inevitable conclusion that a God, defined in our image, is responsible for the unknown (and everything else). If God existed, he, she, or it would not have any justification for refusing to correct the overt inequities on Earth. God, as defined in several different formats by different sects, is a figment of the imagination of one species, on one planet, in one solar system, in one universe, in one fleeting moment. To fight wars and to ostracize neighbors because they define the unknown differently defies logic, experience, and credibility.

In virtually every nation it is socially unacceptable, immoral, and occasionally illegal to advocate that God does not exist. A belief in one definition of God, or the role of Jesus, Buddha, or Mohammed, becomes an integral part of the social fabric providing a security blanket for each coterie of believers. A belief in God, like celebrations of established holidays, affords peace of mind and allows devotees to allot essential time to wars, riots, prejudicial behavior, and the making of money.

Since my country now erroneously exists "under God," in spite of patent constitutional prohibitions, and the Ten Commandments have returned to the schools, I am increasingly alienated by my own society.

If a significant number of citizens had the courage to express the belief that organized religion, with its variable definitions of God, is merely a form of social interaction, jingoism would become less subjective, and the quest for peace might warrant greater attention.

ON THE FIRST DAY

When God was contemplating his agenda for the coming week, why did he decide to create the world? At that time there must have been other priorities that mere mortals are unable to fathom. If God had the power to create the world, he might have selected another option that was more meaningful.

The only viable alternative was for God to appoint a committee to formulate a list of priorities. The committee would still be deliberating and hard rock music and Madonna would never have been invented.

If God really existed, and if he were omnipotent, he would have foreseen that the world he created would not be considered a work of art. If God conjured up the "big bang" that led inevitably to Newt Gingrich, he could have insured a bigger bang with the selection of another option that might have at least represented a bit of fun.

I have no idea what God might have done during the stimulating first seven days other than taking the impressive steps reported in Genesis. If God could contemplate the Immaculate Conception, he might have formulated a system more immaculate than the planet on which we live.

3

HEAVEN AND HELL

Heaven expresses an unattainable dream. Hell represents a living reality. *

A Reservation in Heaven

The Christian concept of Heaven contemplates a figurative green pasture for the people we have known on Earth. For example, when a parent dies, we take solace in the belief that we "will see her in Heaven." That large heavenly pasture must be immense.

If we think realistically about the concept of Heaven, we should recognize that the gigantic pasture beyond the pearly gates must be large enough to provide at least an economy seat for every "good" Christian who ever existed. If we are charitable, a few exemplary non-Christians (who did not have the benefit of exposure to Christian dogma) might also be admitted.

I submit that when I begin the search for my parents in that heavenly place, it might be difficult to find them quickly. Even with a generous dose of ESP, which may inure to the benefit of Christian souls, the search would be onerous. It may be comforting to assume that God will direct each of us to our loved ones and friends in Heaven, but it is more realistic to recognize that God will have more important things to do than providing a travel guide for each new initiate to Heaven.

The Christian answer to this pragmatic issue would be to suggest the Heaven is not a literal "place," and that "seeing" your loved ones might be more figurative than real. On the other hand, it is more likely that my place in Heaven (to which I will be assigned assuming that my lifestyle on Earth changes appreciably) will be shared with millions of coolies from the Ming dynasty. Of course, I am assuming that those coolies were never exposed to Christian missionaries; therefore, they were right-thinking, right-living non-Christians who lacked exposure to the true gospel and did not exercise any unacceptable freedom of choice regarding religion. I am not engaging in raw jingoism. The learning experience (if that exists in Heaven) might be energizing, but unless God is willing to assign me a seat with those with whom I am culturally comfortable, I am uncertain whether loving my neighbor is that big a deal. On second thought, after a lifetime with friends and family, the next life with a multitude of Chinese coolies might be a welcome relief.

REMEMBERING THOSE IN HEAVEN

Behavior while living should not guarantee a place in Heaven. Goodness should only insure access. Once you have arrived in Heaven, the real competition begins. In Heaven, following the Dantean concentric-rings precedent, status will be determined by the frequency with which you are remembered favorably by those remaining on Earth. Quantity should not be the paramount factor. This approach would eliminate celebrity manifestations, cult identification, charisma, and the stuffing of ballot boxes. Crowd adulation would be replaced by the favorable memories of individuals who think for themselves. Obviously, that would limit the sample. It is unlikely that any soul in Heaven would receive more than a handful of favorable memories.

If, during your lifetime, you actually accomplished something worth remembering, the positive thoughts of individual survivors would determine the pecking order in Heaven. The skill of a press agent, or charms of a "backslapper," would be irrelevant. Your own interpretation of your "goodness" would be equally immaterial. If there is only one person who continues to think of you fondly, and that person thinks of you frequently, you will be rewarded in Heaven. In the absence of a definitive Hell, those in Heaven who are remembered with less than sincere, frequent memories will be relegated to a lower tier in Heaven.

I admit that my superior approach to the concept of Heaven presents difficulty with the time variable, but even Einstein grappled with the same problem. Obviously, points can only be earned for a limited period of time. If the memories of President Kennedy begin to swing from negative to positive, after several generations, those ballots would not count. Perspective should have no place in Heaven. Basically, the pecking order in Heaven will be dependent upon the survivors in your generation who knew you well, who think approvingly of you, and who are not exposed to external complexities such as reading or even the media.

Before you discard summarily this novel concept of Heaven, give it a try. Think fondly about a deceased person whom you knew well. Do you not feel better? Does it not stand to reason that if you feel better, and if God is cognizant of your remembrance, that your friend, associate, or family member in Heaven will be blessed? Your favorable evaluation may induce God to place the deceased in a more favorable niche in Heaven.

With this religious credo, those who transgress may get what they deserve. Of greater importance, you cannot buy, bequeath, or euchre your way from one circle to a more prestigious circle in Heaven. The cost of your funeral on Earth will be meaningless. If your good deeds were not actually perceived as such by those who knew you, there will not be any chance for a "high five" in the top rings of Heaven.

AGE OF ENTRY TO HEAVEN

One-third of the American people believe that they will be the same age in Heaven as they are at the time of their deaths. What in Heaven do the other two-thirds believe?

Let's suppose that a large percentage of these religious zealots are convinced that they will have the option of starting over as newborn babes. If I had the option to relive my life, exactly as I have lived it, I would refuse to accept. Also, I would never opt for Heaven with the infirmities that I now enjoy. My mistakes have been legion, and I would rather not be exposed to them again. If I were to start over as somebody else, there are few folks with whom I would trade places for a lifetime.

Only two options remain. Select an age between zero and your current age or cross through the Pearly Gates even older than you are now. The later is preposterous. Who would want to be forced to focus on personal plumbing problems in Heaven? The former makes more sense, but even living a selected year over again would constitute double jeopardy.

It would appear that the only seminal thinkers in the religious fraternity are the one-third who selected their current age for admission to Heaven. Those are the people who are satisfied with their lot, who clip their coupons, who really do not need the benefits of Heaven, and who feel that the rest of us can go to Hell.

One unexplored possibility remains. Two-thirds may feel that they will enter Heaven as ageless spirits. On Earth I have attempted to be an ageless spirit, and I can assure you that the role is difficult. Arthritis has taken my spirit, and I am only ageless when a definitive age really counts (like qualifying for a cocktail, social security, or a starting time at the country club).

RULES IN HEAVEN

It would be reassuring to know that in Heaven we could avoid the defects of societal rules on Earth. Having observed the certitude of religious devotees, and their disdain for proof, I believe as an article of faith (oops, let's just say that I believe) that the religious rules in Heaven would be as confining, irrational, irrelevant, and arcane as those on Earth.

If Heaven exists, it is ridiculous to contemplate that those who have earned access would not be under close scrutiny. If there is more than one soul in Heaven, there would have to be rules most of which would be broken. What sanctions would then be imposed?

It has never been suggested by the religious pundits that those who are admitted to Heaven would be incapable of thought (unless those who think are precluded from entering Heaven). God will want to correct error "on Earth as it is in Heaven." If Hell does not subscribe to religious rules, the heat might be tolerable.

HEAVEN AND HELL

When Earth was considered flat, and Christians believed as they do now, in Heaven and Hell, was Heaven up or down? Clearly, the believers opined, the flat Earth was a floating slab in the universe, or an infinite plane; therefore, "Heaven and Hell" made a modicum of sense. Since you could only see "up," Heaven was above. Assuming that the flat Earth was a slab with indefinite depth, the concept of "down" was lucid. Hell was "down" an unspecified depth.

With Earth in its present shape (structurally, that is), I assume that Heaven is somewhere in the universe in any direction, or in all directions, and that Hell is below somewhere in the core of Earth.

Once again, we have proven that a little learning is dangerous. When we were ignorant, and Earth was adjudged flat, it was relatively easy to be a believer in Heaven and Hell. Now, with a bit of knowledge, we know that Hell cannot be "down" into the finite and limited core of Earth. Heaven and Hell must be "out there" somewhere. They may even reside in the same direction (perish the thought). They might even be in the same locus. If that is the case, why not save time and money for the church offering by enjoying or suffering through both Heaven and Hell while we spend our brief sojourn on Earth?

It is comforting to believe that Heaven and Hell reside in each of us, in variable doses, and that they are always located on Earth's surface at a distance above or below Earth's surface. The only partial exceptions pertain to the astronauts and aquanauts who have taken a bit of both concepts a few thousand miles out into the stratosphere or a few miles down into the ocean depths.

From the moment of birth, humans experience Heaven and Hell. If tomorrow it is established that the universe can be fully explained, organized religion will be forced to invent a new concept for the rewards and punishments of earthly existence.

HELL OF A MESS

Hell is a derivative of the Anglo-Saxon word meaning "to conceal." It was introduced into the Christian vocabulary prior to A.D. 900. The meanings have expanded appreciably. Today, "hell" can refer to postmortem grief, an abode of evil, the home of the damned, bedlam, the depths, a gambling house, a hot place, the nether world, Hades or Sheol, a locus for misery or torment, or a place of confinement. The uses of the word appear to be infinite.

Parts of Speech

Noun

> **hellion**: a troublesome imp
>
> **hell-raiser**: a mature hellion
>
> **hell's bells**: the chimes of irritation
>
> **hellcat**: the other woman
>
> **hell-hole**: an enemy's hostel
>
> **hellishness**: a kitten with sharp claws
>
> **heller**: a noisy person
>
> **Hellenist**: a guy who admires Greeks
>
> **hell broth**: an evil soup
>
> **hell bound**: a fiend
>
> **hell week**: college boy fun
>
> **hello**: a greeting from the devil

Adverb

> hellishly: with verve
> ran like hell: after throwing a snowball
> hate like hell: a hate crime
> the hell you say: you are wrong

Adjective

> hellish: house chores
> hell-for-leather: reckless riding
> hell-bent: painful arthritis
> hell-like: pretty bad
> hellacious: formidable

Pronoun, Adjective, or Adverb

> helluva: mighty big

Fun and Games

hell around: cut up
for the hell of it: a suspect rationale
raise hell: a teenager in action
what the hell: it is not my fault
hell on wheels: the Indy 500
play hell with: a triple bogey

Interrogatories

Where the hell were you?: when the check was presented
Who the hell?: I did not do it

Difficult Circumstances

These roads are hell: the rush hour
come hell or high water: Hobson's Choice
hell of a price: what a deal
She made his life hell: matrimony
to catch hell: worse than a cold
to give someone hell: a gift to be avoided

Places and Things

Hell Gate: East River channel in New York City
Hell's Mouth: entrance to hell
Hell's Kitchen: New York City development
Hell's Canyon: somewhere west of New York City
Hellbrunn Zoo: In Munich, the animals do not seem to care
Hell's Angels: a movie and a juvenile motorcycle group
Hell Diver: a grebe, or an aircraft bomber pilot
Hellfire: a guided missile, or a drinking society in England

A Substitute for Profanity

guilty as hell
hell of a nice guy
the hell with it
go to hell

Hades in Literature

"All hell broke loose": John Milton, *Paradise Lost*
"Black as hell": William Shakespeare, "Sonnet 147"
"Hot as hell": Charles Maurice de Tallyrand-Perigord, "Recipe of Coffee"
"Into the mouth of hell": Alfred, Lord Tennyson, "The Charge of the Light Brigade"
"Italy (is) hell for women": Robert Burton, *Anatomy of Melancholy*
"What in hell have I done": Donald Robert Perry Maquis, "mehitabel and her kittens"
"War is hell": William Tecumseh Sherman, *National Tribune*
"till hell freezes": anonymous
"Tell him to go to hell": Zachary Taylor, "Reply to Santa Ana's Surrender Ultimatum"
"print the news and raise hell": *Chicago Times*
"Hell is paved with good intentions": John Ray, "English Proverbs"
"It would be hell on earth": George Bernard Shaw, *Man and Superman*
"nor hell a fury like woman scorned": William Congreve, "The Morning Bride"
Lillian Hellman, "Toys in the Attic": (she rose above gender and surname)

Variable Sectarian Approaches

Norse: hell was a celestial residence for souls of all shades.
Pueblo Indians: all of the dead become clouds
Prophet religions: a dwelling place for the damned
    Christianity: a fiery domain for the unrepentant
    Islam: a huge crater of fire
    Zoroastrianism: a freezing domain
    Hinduism: twenty-one hells in the career of the soul with eventual return to the world
    Buddhism: multiple hells in the cosmic realm

The concepts of Hell appear to be infinite. In *The Divine Comedy*, Dante interposed purgatory between Heaven and Hell as a staging ground on the journey to Hell or to Paradise.

A more pragmatic response would be to suggest that Heaven should be eliminated. In Hell, there is a greater need for service. If a person leads an exemplary existence on Earth, that person should be rewarded with service to the damned in Hell rather than joining the ranks of the unemployed in Heaven.

If a profane word has been selected rather than "hell," a writer might enjoy "a hell of a time."

MIRACLES AND NATURE

4

*Miracles are never justified rationally.**

WATER TO WINE

In the Book of John, there are seven alleged miracles. At a marriage ceremony at Cana in Galilee the available wine was consumed early in the festivities. Jesus and his disciples were in attendance. Mary, the mother of Jesus, requested a miracle. She wanted six thirty-gallon jars that were filled with water to be converted to wine.

The response of Jesus reflected justifiable exasperation with his maternal parent: "O'Woman, What have you to do with me? My hour has not yet come!" Transcending his temporary pique, Jesus converted the water to wine. The product was superior to the cheap batch of wine served by the host. This is the first miracle performed by Jesus as recorded by John.

A few questions come to mind:

◈ After consuming 180 gallons of wine, which guests would have the sobriety to report accurately? In subsequent gospels, none of the other disciples, who were present at the reception, commented on the incident, and there is not any indication that the guests or the servants gave testimony following the event.

◈ Mary's goading of her son was intemperate and not particularly maternal. Since we cannot authenticate when the Book of John was written, the lapse of years may have provoked a margin of error or (perish the thought) even a slight fabrication.

◈ If Jesus was convinced that "his hour had not yet come," why did he perform the miracle? At the ceremony, he did not provide an explanation.

◈ If no prior miracle had been performed, why was Mary confident that Jesus could comply, particularly for such a mundane purpose? If Jesus had been "my son, the doctor," Mary would not have ordered a medical miracle on the spot.

◈ There is not any natural means to change water into wine. For the host at a wedding reception to run out of wine does not constitute a major emergency. What was Jesus proving and for whom? Why not provide food and drink for the entire community while he was in the mood?

◈ The initial miracle reflects a meaningless gesture in the lap of luxury. Jesus was not prone to engage in meaningless gestures. Why did not Jesus honor his own caveat regarding timeliness and defer the first miracle for a more propitious occasion?

The evidence against the performance of a miracle on this occasion is preponderant. If John's "water to wine" story was confirmed by at least one other witness or reporter, and if Jesus had tied the miracle to a bit of scripture, there might be a few more believers.

LOURDES

Emile Zola placed the miracle cures commemorated at Lourdes in perspective. He inquired why wooden legs were not discovered among the crutches of those who had been (ostensibly) cured.

HUMAN FACES

For a lifetime, I have repudiated miracles. Now, I recognize that I see at least a score every day.

Each human face is different. With six billion people residing on Earth, not one of us has ever witnessed two identical faces (with the possible exception of a set of unusual identical twins, and that in itself is a miracle).

There are "look alike" contests to emulate Elvis Presley, but the similarities are confined to hairstyle and color, clothes, and the hip movements, rather than physiogomy. The infinite variety of facial features presents an endless exposure to miracles in action.

A LUNAR ECLIPSE

One evening, we were delighted to observe the relatively rare total eclipse. The phenomenon occurs every twenty years. The Moon appeared to be abnormally large, and the effect lasted for more than two hours. From our vantage point above the ocean, the eclipse was exceptionally beautiful. Through the scope, we were able to enjoy it in elaborate detail.

A lunar eclipse occurs when the Moon travels through the shadow of Earth. At that moment, the Moon is not illuminated by the Sun because of the Earth's shadow. The rare total lunar eclipse only occurs when the Moon passes through the center of Earth's shade, which creates a perfect shadow. A lunar eclipse takes place only when there is a full Moon (when the Moon is directly opposite from the Sun).

When you gaze at a total lunar eclipse, it is easy to relate to the ancient mystical beliefs that were provoked by its rarity. Without the benefit of scientific knowledge, the devised rationale could easily endorse the work of a god or goddess expressing displeasure with mere mortals. Science has removed the exotic, mystical component but not the romantic appeal of a total eclipse of the Moon.

A TREE**

I am deeply grateful to God (and to Joyce Kilmer) for creating the tree. Sit for a moment and watch a tree, and you will rise to the occasion.

When the leaves blow to honor the wind, I dream of travel. When the leaves are still, I dream of ideas yet unborn. When the leaves fall, I dream of lost opportunities. When the buds appear, I dream of unfulfilled promise.

A tree can be older than I and infinitely wiser. A garden tree can be younger than I and dependent upon my pruning lore. A tree in the forest inspires, but ignores, my love.

When the Sun is maddening, a tree provides essential solace. When the rain falls, a tree serves as my umbrella. When the birds require a home, a tree complies.

In winter, when the leaves have departed, the branches of a tree prompt awe and introspection. Even a fallen tree enjoys a state of grace.

If only God can make a tree, he deserves a star for good work. If he would caution the loggers, I would recommend a second star.

MOON OVER MISQUAMICUT**

Last night, as I was running on a road adjoining the salt pond, the Moon emerged over the water. The greater intensity of the winter Sun created an orange cast that engulfed the Moon and extended through the shimmering, icy water. Grayish black clouds crossed in front of the Moon obscuring the craters that formerly depicted the facial features of a man. In the freezing air, a great blue heron croaked as he or she headed for another fishing station; the herring gulls cried over each other; the cormorants voiced displeasure with their wintry bath, and the Canada geese broke ranks to land for an evening's rest.

The light of the full Moon was sufficient to see the outline of the trees on the distant pond shore, and a cold wind moaned across the stillness of an incandescent lagoon.

Within minutes, the Moon had risen beyond the Sun's rosy grasp, and the pallid white glow reminded me of winters past. The birds were roosting, and smoke from neighbors' fireplaces evoked nostalgia rather than ecological concern.

Winter can depress the spirits and cause pain in the joints, but the qualitative seasonal variation stimulates perspective, sporadic joy, and a recognition that life is cyclical as well as fleeting.

A human footprint on the Moon did not impinge upon esthetics. It only created wariness about spatial debris. Inevitably, humanity will approach a complete understanding of nature, but a full, wintry Moon over water represents faith as well as fact. The poets and composers can describe Earth's sole satellite with special skill—beam, glow, paper, shine, silvery, and struck—but I can still become "moony" when the full version does its thing over an expanse of frigid water.

Restraints on sin result from societal pressure rather than religious credo.*

SIN AND SOCIETY

I believe that sin is unacceptable. Unless it is punished, or at least discouraged, the fabric of society is in jeopardy. Sin is not confined to the guidelines of scripture. It is defined by the leadership of cults, nations, and societies. When two nations or societies endorse a different concept of sin, chaos may result.

Fortunately, in most societies, heinous crimes such as murder and rape are subject to maximum punishment. In the absence of war, such sins are discouraged or at least subject to incarceration.

For lesser crimes, or antisocial activities, society decrees that lesser sentences, including ostracism, will be levied. Societal norms dictate the deterrence not the prohibitions from religious scripture.

Since time immemorial, people have abjured sin out of fear of retribution from the society with which they are affiliated, not out of fear of violating religious credo. Natural law is merely refined codification of social norms that were created to nurture a secure social environment. If Gods had not been invented, there would not be any need to cast sin in the context of religious infraction. The Ten Commandments reflect common sense, not the word of God.

SLOTH

Having recently seen a number of three-toed sloths in the wild, I regret that the intriguing creature has gotten a bum rap.

In various dictionaries, sloth is defined as "indolence, laziness or avoiding labor or activity." The second meaning of "sloth" is a slow-moving, arboreal mammal that hangs "upside down" (with its back facing the ground might be a more accurate description).

Since the word "sloth" was not coined in a behavioral sense until the twelfth century, it is a bit disconcerting that Thomas Aquinas sealed the negative perception of this innocuous mammal by incorporating "sloth" as the last of the seven "deadly" or cardinal sins. It is also odd that a rather scarce animal that is domiciled from Honduras to northern Brazil would strike the fancy of an eventual saint residing in Italy.

It is pertinent to note that the definitive list of "deadly sins" was formulated in the sixth century, long before the minions of Columbus might have seen the hapless creature and taken one back to Spain for the enjoyment of royalty. "Deadly" was employed because each of the infractions or "sins" might escalate to the others.

The writers of Exodus did not consider "sloth" of sufficient importance to warrant inclusion in the Ten Commandments, but I suppose that "lust" and "coveting your neighbor's man servant" were of sufficient importance to justify emphasis. In any event, St. Thomas Aquinas considered spiritual apathy or inactivity the equivalent of sloth, which has insured that the bulk of humankind has been violating the seventh "deadly sin."

A closer look at the offensive sloth discloses a creature with limited eyesight and hearing. For survival it is dependent upon an acute sense of touch. Since its bone structure is inadequate, its musculature is limited. The stomach constitutes 30 percent of the body weight, and since the sloth cannot walk, the diet is confined to the leaves of the cecropia tree, which also serves as its home.

Since the sloth's digestive process is slow it remains in a tree for three to eight days, only descending to the base to perform critical bodily functions. If a sloth desires to have dinner in a nearby cecropia, it must crawl on the ground by pulling its body forward with its claws.

With limited sight and hearing, nature has designed a unique protective coloration for the sloth. When it hangs from a limb, it resembles a clump of dead leaves. Because it is physiologically incapable of rapid motion, its slowness in moving along a limb affords protection against predators.

Because of an imperfect temperature control system, a change to a colder climate transforms the sloth into a torpid state that St. Thomas Aquinas might have considered "slothful."

It is fortunate that the sloth has a thick skin. Without that feature, it might not have the courage to hang on when the Christian sermons are broadcast. On the other hand, hearing defects can be advantageous.

Before leaving the subject, I should extend my apologies to St. Thomas Aquinas. The word "sloth" was not in use in England until the twelfth century. Since Aquinas lived from 1224 until 1274, and since knowledge of the sloth could not have been known in Europe for three more centuries, he must be excused from guilt.

There are four Latin words that depict the slothful condition. The French word "slouthe" was obviously derived from the English (or vice versa), and the Spanish word "perezoso" has escaped the list of sins.

Since Aquinas is off the hook, we must now identify the culprit who applied the word "sloth" to the mammal. A scientist with the surname Brady has his name assigned to the sloth family (Bradypodidae) and species (*bradypus*), but the blackguard who did the job on the sloth is lost in anonymous infamy.

In the near future, I will enlighten you with the derivation of the word "lust."

EVE AND SIN

There are two fables that explain the origin of Adam and Eve. The first alleges that they sprang forth together. Because that version is seldom cited, it can be ignored. The most ridiculous version discusses Adam's rib as the point of Eve's departure. Imagine Adam waiting fourteen years (plus or minus a few years) for Eve to mature physically. The origin of the first sin represents an equally suspect exposition.

According to an unknown, hallucinating ancient author, Eve yielded to the temptations of an evil serpent in the Garden of Eden and convinced Adam that they should both eat the forbidden fruit. Their diet prior to this remarkable event has never been described. It is hard to believe that an apple is more forbidden that a pomegranate.

Eve's indiscretion in consuming the fruit represents, for true believers, the first documented sin. The snake and Adam are exonerated from this bit of sinful behavior. For the moment, we must ignore Adam's "original sin," which was innate and which we have all ostensibly inherited.

Now my main point emerges. As punishment, God bestowed upon Eve, and all women, pain in childbirth and subordination to the masculine gender. At the same time, God decided to practice equity by decreeing that Adam's fall from grace should require all of humankind (excluding women) to toil for subsistence. Childbirth and child care might be considered toil, but let's not play with words.

At the risk of perdition, a person might be tempted to accuse God of male chauvinism. Listening to a serpent (in any language) is no more sinful than eating tainted fruit. Adam and Eve were equally guilty; yet, Eve received unusual punishment that reflected her child-bearing proclivities rather than the nature of her infraction.

This fable implies that woman's exclusive responsibility for childbirth was launched by God without corresponding pain. When God assigned childbirth to women, the toil part of the equation was automatically man's burden (at least until the late twentieth century when women were granted permission "to toil for subsistence").

Historical revisionism is always suspect, but I do believe that God was a bit prejudiced in designating Eve as the first sinner. If this fable is true, God must have been masculine.

THE UNIVERSE

6

*Religion imposes a
subjective interpretation
of the unknown.**

GOD BEFORE GOD

I t is difficult to avoid the subject of religion in a society addicted to
television, a medium that provides unlimited access to religious fundamentalists. Have you noticed that fundamentalists do not wrestle
with the question of what occupied the attention of God prior to his or
her creation of Earth (or to allow for revisionism) before the creation of
the universe?

If the magnitude of the currently observable universe extends for
one plus twenty-four zeros, as measured in miles, there must have been
a large chunk of pre-universal space that God supervised prior to the
creation of the universe.

Since I am way out on a limb, and only God can grow a tree, it
would be dishonest to fail to inquire about what existed before the creation of God. I realize that I am engaged in nonsanctioned thought, but
with the problems that humankind has faced since Adam and Eve, there
must have been a power greater than God that did an inadequate job in
creating an error-prone God.

47

Before relinquishing the floor, may I opine that part of the problem is related to the fact that science confines its inquiry to the nature and extent of the universe and when it was created. When scientists allot time to answering "why" there is a universe, there may be a partial answer to religious certitude and hypocrisy.

SCIENCE AND RELIGION

Antimatter

I am fascinated by the scientific concept of antimatter. My knowledge of physics is certifiably inadequate, but from the layman's point of view, I am intrigued by a thesis that may explain the origin of the universe. If for every force there is a counterforce, the "big bang" thesis may gain credibility. The Asian philosophical concept of Yin and Yang, with their rationale related to counterforces, may be closer to the mark than the incredible allegations in Genesis (no matter how many times it is revised and/or updated).

The "Big Bang"

If Albert Einstein, Stephen Hawking, and their scientific colleagues have been unable to describe the void that existed prior to the "big bang," we should not expect self-appointed religious Messiahs, promoters, or quacks to fill the void (if you will pardon the expression).

If the "big bang" created time, space, energy, and matter, the Garden of Eden and Noah's Ark might be suspect. On the other hand, a void is a void, and it, too, has an origin.

Quasars

"Quasar" is a word that did not appear in the dictionary until 1964, and yet it has induced scientists to redefine the concept of the universe. Research now suggests that we must extend the distance between Earth and the unknown. We now understand more about the distant universe, but we seldom even conjecture about the unknown beyond the identified universe.

It is patently clear that religion, in all of its manifestations, is irrelevant in attempting to explain the void in space. It is tempting, and undoubtedly simplistic, to suggest that as telescopes become more powerful, people will see themselves while looking through a telescope into space. In that event, the universe would either be round or a mirror of itself. If it were round, what would sustain the universe? If it were merely a reflection, what would account for the reflection?

It is obvious that the universe is still incomprehensible in size, scope, and content. It is also obvious that any concept of God has about as much to do with the issue as the "Man in the Moon." The pseudoscientists and fundamentalists who argue that each new scientific discovery further substantiates a religious credo are ignoring an essential verity. Humankind will explain the unknown or destroy the universe in the process.

PERCEPTION OF THE UNIVERSE

In a few centuries our understanding of the universe has evolved fundamentally. In the process the romantic component has disappeared.

In the age of Ptolemy, the universe was explained by geocentric cosmologies that were as fictitious as religious tenets but created a comparable partisan fervor. Copernicus and Galileo devised a heliocentric cosmology that concentrated correctly on the solar system but did not shed light on broader universal profundities.

Today, we are informed that Earth is rather a lackluster, medium-sized planet that orbits around a Sun that is in reality a rather mundane star. The galaxy to which Earth has been assigned is one of millions in the universe. When the scope of the universe is further increased, through sophisticated instrumentation, the number of galaxies will multiply astronomically (to coin a phrase).

With the discovery of "black holes," the remarkable improvement of telescopes, and the data generated by scientifically oriented satellites, the universe is gradually becoming a scientific laboratory rather than a lovely void on which dreams and religious credos are based.

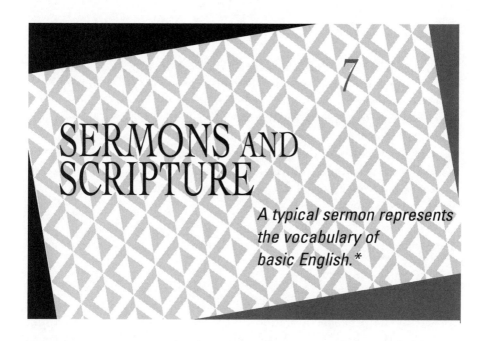

SERMONS AND SCRIPTURE

7

A typical sermon represents the vocabulary of basic English.*

THE GOSPEL OF LUKE

A t a recent church service the preacher made a number of startling comments about the Gospel according to Luke. I was
motivated to reread the biblical source. Assuming that Luke was
responsible for the third book in the New Testament (substantial doubt
exists about his authorship), he was the only Gentile whose Gospel
appears in the Bible. Luke wrote for the Gentiles, not for the Jews. To
illustrate, he traces the ultimate progenitor of Christ to Adam not to the
Jewish "father."

Luke relates the story of the life and death of Jesus. Although half
of his work was borrowed from Mark, Luke's Gospel is the only source
for the circumstances surrounding the Ascension and the parables of
the Good Samaritan and the Prodigal Son.

I am dismayed by the force, the lack of documentation, and the bel-
ligerent tone of the doctrine. In most of the New Testament the reader
may disagree with the content, but generally it is gentle, harmless, and
easy to ignore. In contrast, the Gospel of Luke is the antithesis of peace

and reasonableness. For example, Luke urges us to hate the members of our family, if circumstances warrant, and to take indiscriminately all possessions from the rich and distribute them to the poor. Luke's concepts are unique and alien. When reading Luke, I am angry, not just bored, as I am with the typical meaningless and innocuous dogma.

If Christ had read the Book of Luke (Luke was not a disciple), he would have disowned the doctrine. Luke does not "turn the other cheek"; he buries his quill deep into the perception of Jesus Christ as teacher and healer.

GOD ASKS QUESTIONS

At a local summer chapel, the guest preacher, the epitome of a "yuppie," stressed the theme that God asks questions rather than providing answers. The preacher admitted that God had only interrogated him once directly. He did not share with the congregation the manner in which he answered God. The sermon was banal, devoid of substance and dull.

At a neighborhood reception following the service, I inquired whether the preacher had considered expanding the sermon's theme to include the possibility that the sinner might ask himself or herself critical questions before relying upon higher authority. The preacher informed me that the idea was "interesting," and he volunteered the non sequitur that he had delivered the same sermon to his home congregation.

This is the extent of my exploration into the arcane skill of preparing religious sermons. It would appear that if you ask a believer to attempt to answer his or her own question, he or she might volunteer a partial answer. Since scripture contains all of the answers, only God is allowed to ask questions.

SERMONS AND VOCABULARY

As a teenager, I would entertain my parents by presenting an impromptu religious sermon utilizing the appropriate words of art. The words flowed. The tirade might last for five minutes. The content did not differ appreciably from the fundamentalist sermons that were then heard exclusively on the radio. If I now attempted to repeat the performance, it would be impossible. What has changed?

First, the spoken word precedes words spoken with meaning. Substantive articulation requires maturity of judgment accompanied by an expanding vocabulary. Young people are capable of mimicking. That is why children learn foreign languages with dispatch. It is relatively easy to repeat the commonplace words and thoughts associated with most sermons.

Second, self-confidence is a minimal factor. Although the occasion may not demand it, a teenager can rise to the occasion. When you are not forced to think, the words flow.

Third, as an only child, in the absence of television, such performances provided a modicum of entertainment at the dinner table.

Finally, many young people possess a knack for making a speech. As you mature, preparation is essential because the audience and the subject matter become more complex. The vocabulary required for a normal sermon barely exceeds basic English, and even five hundred words may be stretching the point. Occasionally, a sermon may display content, but a diligent search is required.

If you feel that this essay constitutes a condemnation of the typical sermon, you caught my drift.

PAGAN LOVE

In the first book of John in the New Testament, chapter 4, verse 7 (even citing the passage without the prescribed structure provides a sense of independence), it is alleged: "Beloved, let us love one another; for love is of God; and everyone that loveth is born of God, and knoweth God."

That biblical reference reflects the epitome of religious arrogance. According to the New Testament, if I do not believe in God, I am incapable of love. How can Christians be exposed to such hyperbole and not rebel?

God, if there is a God, would not insist that those who have not been exposed to his grace, or the scripture that allegedly interprets him, could not love. For those who have not been introduced to the concept of God, in the Christian sense, God would recognize that love can exist even where that love is not "born of God."

Since the beginning of time (for *Homo sapiens*), human beings lived from the utilization of fire to the birth of Christ with love in their hearts. Love is the result of meaningful human interaction, not the divine intervention of God. Love incorporates tenderness (on occasion), feeling, appreciation, physical attraction, a sense of well-being in the presence of another person over an extended period of time (usually exceeding one night), or any combination of the above.

If the early African explorers had been pagan, and the resident black savages had been Christian, the last century of the evolution of the Christian doctrine might have presented a revised concept of love.

If Christians believe that Christian love differs from generic love, Christianity becomes an even more divisive force. To be informed that we cannot love unless we believe in the Christian interpretation of God is blasphemy. Everyone who is privileged to live is not a believer in the unique Christian version of God.

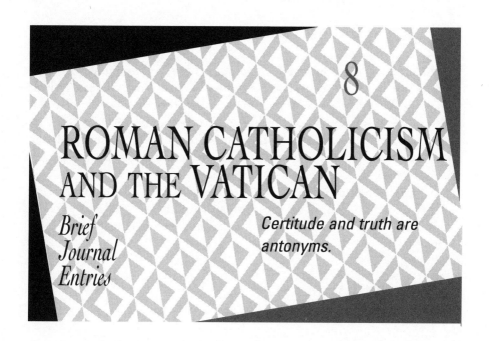

ROMAN CATHOLICISM AND THE VATICAN

Brief Journal Entries

Certitude and truth are antonyms.

PAPAL VESTMENTS (SEPTEMBER 1983)

Following the assassination attempt of Pope John Paul II, it was announced that the pope was sporting a bulletproof vest. I am tempted to wax philosophical about the alleged vulnerability of the vicar of Christ; however, I recognize that my failure to accept the faith may be considered prejudicial. If the pope is required to wear a bullet-proof vest, I am certain that the pundits in the Vatican can concoct another implausible theory, which is not subject to proof, to convince millions of Catholics that corporal vulnerability is, in reality, the invulnerability of faith.

After all, these are the same wise men who convinced the Latino faithful that birth control by rhythm warrants God's blessing while the lowly condom violates the holy scriptures. Remember, also, that the leadership in the Vatican embraced National Socialism, has not yet recognized that Gallileo was correct in describing the physical implications of falling objects, and has allowed a Polish pope to intervene in Polish politics.

Since I am not competent to fathom these unfathomables, I must restrict my commentary to laic concerns. In New York State, a culprit who commits a felony while wearing a bulletproof vest is now charged with an aggravated crime. In other words, if a crook protects himself from gun-bearing honest citizens, he is guilty of a greater crime. If the vicar of Christ protects himself from a comparable threat, the pope's decrees should not be considered relevant.

From this analysis, if a criminal in New York State wears a priest's robe while committing a felony, Galileo should be eligible to join the National Rifle Association. What a seamless web true believers do weave!

THE POPE IN AFRICA (AUGUST 1985)

Pope John Paul II has concluded a triumphant tour of black Africa. His visit should have been reported as the "Manifest Damage of Catholicism." Imagine the counterproductive impact when the pope opposes birth control and abortion but defends the Catholic concept of "the unbreakable union of husband and wife" in a culture that has endorsed multiple wives for at least a millennium and predates the advent of Catholicism. He suggests that environmental problems should be evaluated "in relation to the needs of actual men and women," yet he issues an appeal on behalf of the victims of famine (without helping to resolve the food shortage), and criticizes apartheid (while creating an equally objectionable form of apartheid between Catholics and the rest of society).

When the most important religious figure in the world ignores black Africa's most serious problem (overpopulation); condemns the tribal marital customs that reflect a historic rationale; ignores indigenous religious beliefs; and suggests that environmental controls are only acceptable when they will not have adverse impact on living human beings, the future of black Africa is in jeopardy. In practical terms, the pope has advocated that Africans have large families that cannot be adequately fed; that Africans denude the landscape for firewood, which increases desert areas and provokes more famine; that they ignore their traditional local customs; and that they join the Catholic Church.

At a critical time the Polish pope was needed in Poland as an antidote to the Soviet brand of communism. In Africa, he is not needed to promote a series of alleged reforms that will exacerbate current conditions and destroy viable historic mores. In one short African tour, the pope has undone the work of legions of committed human beings, including missionaries, who have made important strides in development, conservation, population control, and the quality of life. At some point, religious zealots must be held accountable. Freedom of religion may be lost when religious advocates engage in conversion techniques that are devoid of a factual base and a knowledge of local beliefs and conditions.

THE WORLD'S LARGEST CHRISTIAN CHURCH (MARCH 1989)

Cote d'Ivoire in West Africa is a nation of approximately fifteen million people. The overwhelming majority profess animistic beliefs; one-fourth are Muslim, and one-fifth endorse Roman Catholicism. One hundred and forty miles east of the capital of Abidjan is the city of Yamoussoukro, the birthplace of Felix Houphouet-Boigny. In 1960, Houphouet-Boigny became the first president of the newly independent Ivory Coast. Subsequently, the name of the country was changed to Cote d'Ivoire to insure that their United Nations representatives would not be forced to sit next to those from Israel.

President Houphouet-Boigny decided to build the largest Christian Church in the world in his old hometown. From 1986 to 1989, a Roman Catholic Cathedral was constructed with seemingly unlimited funds provided by the president (and unwittingly, major donor countries in the West). The basilica is based on the format of St. Peter's in Rome with a large plaza in the front encircled by two colonnades. The cathedral features 271 Doric columns that rise to 101 feet and a dome that dwarfs St. Peter's. Over 18,000 worshipers can be accommodated inside the cathedral. A crowd of 300,000 can assemble comfortably in and around the plaza (10 percent of the Catholics in Cote d'Ivoire).

In 1990, after thirty years as president, Houphouet-Boigny was reelected in the first openly contested presidential election in Cote d'Ivoire. The president died in December 1997. His body was displayed in the cathedral for two months. For the funeral, the presidents of France and Lebanon and twenty African nations attended.

If a public official saves a significant portion of his or her salary, miracles can occur.

THE POPE IN OUAGADOUGOU (FEBRUARY 1990)

The itinerant pope is visiting five of the poorest countries in West Africa. In Burkino Faso, he advocated increasing development assistance to Africa rather than pouring additional resources into the emerging democracies in eastern Europe.

As a person with Polish roots, the pope is aware that a free eastern Europe will receive extensive internal and external support. Internally, in each country, the resources generated by the Catholic Church will be devoted to rebuilding the influence of the Church, and national educational, cultural, and technological levels of attainment will insure rapid recovery. Western Europe and the United States, with common traditions and related economic goals, will facilitate eastern Europe's quest for modernity. In that context, the pope's general commitment to African development is positive; however, the context for potential support is suspect.

On the day following his plea for increased aid from the West, the pope reiterated the position of the Catholic Church regarding the maintenance of "natural" family relationships including abstinence from any form of artificial birth control. With that statement, he invalidated his previous appeal for greater assistance to poverty-stricken Africa.

In the United States, private philanthropy supports planned parenthood programs in Africa. At the same time, the U.S. government refuses to endorse the utilization of taxpayer dollars for birth-control efforts in the developing world. It is equally ludicrous for the pope to oppose birth-control measures in Africa, where the exploding populations will make all other development assistance measures meaningless, while advocating greater development assistance. Unless planned parenthood is an integral part of the internal development assistance rationale for Africa, the favorable impact of other Western aid ventures will be drowned in a sea of new faces. To recommend increased aid from the developed countries, without pegging that assistance to birth-control programs, will only increase the African population without alleviating general suffering.

With one speech in Ouagadougou, the pope undermined every

other development program, disparaged the few African leaders who have manifested the courage to support planned parenthood, and reduced the potential for creating effective multilateral and regional aid programs in sub-Saharan Africa.

The solution to the external aid dilemma in Africa is easy to formulate but virtually impossible to implement. The magic formula requires good will, a charitable intent, generous resources, a willingness to cooperate with others, and the absence of jingoism. In other words, the United States must take the United Nations seriously; encourage committed Americans to become international civil servants; pay United Nations arrearages; support multilateral efforts where resources are devoted to solving real problems without regard to which nation receives credit; attempt to convince the Catholic Church to alter the meaningless dogma regarding birth control; and make a sustained effort to coordinate private agency involvement in Africa.

Since not one of these objectives is currently feasible, in the absence of political courage, we can only watch in despair when an impoverished leper reaches for the pope's robes in Guinea-Bissau and is presented with a $100 bill by a sympathetic papal aide. That manifestation of development assistance was the equivalent of one-third of the annual per capital income in Guinea-Bissau. If $100 had been devoted to birth control, the positive impact would have been geometric.

THE CATHOLIC CHURCH AND VIOLENCE (JANUARY 1995)

The Catholic bishops of the United States have made public the startling revelation that the United States has created a "culture of violence," and they have issued a call for action. The examples cited are even more startling: "The way people drive; venom spewed on talk shows; brutal political campaigns; the denigration of women in porno movies, and the barbarism of assisted suicide."

The gentle Catholic bishops have done violence to the cause. Contemporary ethics in driving an automobile may not illustrate the Golden Rule in action, but the other carefully selected "violent" cultural traits are *de minimus* representations of Catholic dogma related to the role of women and euthanasia. I am unaware of any religious credo that forbids rough political campaigning or malicious talk on television.

The essence of violence—crimes against the person (assaults, rapes, stabbings, and shootings)—does merit a reference in the concern of the Catholic bishops. An argument can be advanced that violence originates in the home, but the Catholic bishops have failed to incorporate any facts that substantiate a contemporary culture of violence (although in fact, it does exist). In the United States, we live in a violent culture, but the Catholic bishops failed to identify the real culprits.

Violent words and images denoting violence may prove to be precursors of violent action. Before that correlation has been established, we must focus on the education of the citizenry, and the protection of the person, rather than jousting with windmills. When the representatives of the Catholic Church cite the evils of excessive drinking, the molestation of youth, and the health hazard of the rhythm method of birth control as important manifestations of violence, coupled with the gun and the hand, I will take cognizance of their self-serving assertion that violence has become the distinguishing characteristic of American culture. Greed and the preoccupation with "things" might warrant a casual reference.

THE IMMACULATE CONCEPTION (AUGUST 1995)

In A.D. 431, the Vatican declared that Mary was the Mother of God. The Church opined that Mary could not commit sinful acts because of God's grace, and that Mary's acts per se were irrelevant.

The doctrine of the Immaculate Conception was then complete. Mary, the Mother of Jesus, was considered free of "original sin" from the first instant of her conception. This belief did not achieve the status of dogma until the twelfth century, approximately seven hundred years after the Blessed Virgin was declared the Mother of God. In 1854, seven hundred years after the doctrine of Original Sin was formulated, Pope Pius IX, in a papal bull revealed by God, declared that the Immaculate Conception must be believed by all Catholics.

Now that the derivation of the belief in the Immaculate Conception has been clarified, I will begin the research that will accentuate some of the major inconsistencies between the Book of Genesis and modern science.

WOMEN AS CATHOLIC PRIESTS
(DECEMBER 1995)

The Vatican has announced that the ban on female priests is now considered "infallible" doctrine. When the doctrine of infallibility is invoked, the Catholic Church cannot err with regard to the subject matter involved.

For any member of the Catholic Church to remain affiliated after this pronouncement defies understanding. Even secular clubs can no longer bar women from membership. If the Catholic Church wants to restrict the priesthood to men, that is its privilege. In time, if the thesis is adjudged in error, it can be corrected. To decree that this tenuous, topical, societal doctrine cannot be proven faulty, makes a mockery of the concept of "infallibility."

CATHOLIC TRANSUBSTANTIATION
(JUNE 1996)

Holy Communion or the Eucharist is a revered Christian sacrament. At the Last Supper with his disciples, Jesus reputedly said, in a moment of candor, "this (bread) is my body and this (wine) is my blood."

For centuries, the Catholic Church has decreed that the wafers and colored water served at Holy Communion, through the doctrine of transubstantiation, become the actual flesh and blood of Christ. The other Christian sects have not yet received the message, and they treat Communion as a symbolic gesture.

The Quakers are the only perverts in the Christian panoply of sects. The Friends have discontinued the rite of Communion.

If you believe in the doctrine of transubstantiation, you can also believe that the Serb leaders who committed war crimes can retain their membership in the Catholic Church.

THE JESUITS AND IGNORANCE
(SEPTEMBER 1997)

In the Dark Ages, the Jesuits coined a remarkable phrase: "invincible ignorance." The Jesuits applied the concept to the pagan masses. If the phrase had also been applied to the Jesuits, a few religious conflicts might have been minimized.

In the Dark Ages, I am certain that some pagan wanted to respond "With the Jesuits, hubris exceeds ignorance."

ETRUSCANS AND THE POPE (AUGUST 1998)

The Etruscans, who predated the Romans in Italy several centuries before the birth of Christ, believed that manifestations of their deities resided in the livers of animals. Representatives of the Etruscan clergy carefully dissected the liver to establish verities pertaining to their Gods.

Twenty-five centuries later, the clergy have restricted their dissection to a figurative probe of the impressionable minds of the congregation. It would be more palatable to endorse the tangible interpretations of the Etruscan priests than the pope's interpretation of the scriptures pertaining to birth-control techniques, the Immaculate Conception, and women in the priesthood.

OCEANIA AND THE VATICAN (FEBRUARY 1999)

Cardinal Ratzinger, the pope's "top theologian," is convening a conference in San Francisco to "better understand the reality of the religious situation in North America and Oceania." In reality, the agenda is confined to bringing the Vatican message pertaining to "feminism and homosexuality" to the bishops who serve in the United States, Canada, and Australia. The Vatican has not been infallible in pontificating about homosexuality et al. Now, it would appear that a geography lesson might prove useful.

If I were a bishop from "down under" (good heavens), I would resent the inclusion of Australia in the definition of Oceania. Today, the standard definition is confined to approximately 10,000 islands in the Pacific Ocean. Occasionally, in the nineteenth century, Oceania did include Australasia.

When the San Francisco conference has been concluded, we should be able to identify the problems of feminism in Tahiti and Guam.

THE POPE AND RU 486
(JULY 1999)

The pope has denounced the French approved birth-control pill, RU 486, as the "pill of Cain—the monster that kills its brothers."

PAPAL INDULGENCES
(SEPTEMBER 1999)

In 1998, Pope John Paul II, in commemoration of the Holy Year 2000, issued a decree allowing local bishops to bestow "special indulgences for sin." The decree supports a seven-century tradition by offering indulgences during special Church years. A few of the suggested winners are abstinence from drinking or smoking for at least one day, contribution to a charity (amount unspecified), or a brief pilgrimage to a sacred spot. Also, a sinner who has resorted to confessionals will be afforded a reduction of punishment.

This month, the Vatican released a revised manual on indulgences providing additional approaches to forgiveness for Catholics expressing their faith. The last version of the manual was issued a quarter of a century ago.

The manual cites a few actions that might qualify for indulgence. A Vatican official who is a specialist in indulgences suggested that "a factory worker, surrounded by colleagues cursing and using off-color language, courageously makes the sign of the cross." It was also suggested that indulgences might be earned by "public testimony of one's faith in certain circumstances of daily life."

Martin Luther, the founder of the Lutheran sect, rebelled against the granting of indulgences for unimportant or prejudicial reasons. In the twenty-first century, Lutherans allege that salvation is dependent upon God's grace per se while Catholics are able to secure indulgences for minor concessions.

If comparable prizes were awarded by civil authorities to nonbelievers, e.g., waiver of a parking fine, the favorable impact on the incidence of indiscretion might be comparable. To curtail the impact of sin requires willpower, a commitment to the public weal, and appropriate sanctions, rather than a lollipop from the local bishop.

THE POPE AND ABORTION
(OCTOBER 1999)

The antiabortion faction represents a strange lot. In Italy, where there are more Catholics than residents, abortion practices do not provoke the ire of the believing masses. In contrast, in the United States, where the Catholics are a decided minority, even among those who declare their religious preference, the right-to-life forces are violent and omnipresent.

The explanation for the disparity relates to culture. In Europe, violence is generally restrained (because of the learning process of living in close proximity to others in a small space). In the United States, where freedom is considered license and where additional population does not present a comparable threat, religious beliefs are not only worn on the sleeve, but they can also lead to violence. More important, nonsectarian fundamentalism can beget agitators who believe in life for the fetus even though religious principles may not be the primary motivation.

Only in the United States can planned parenthood be perceived as the major thrust of the international program of the United Nations. For once, it would appear that the Vatican is not the leading culprit. On the other hand, the Catholic Church is a major player in curtailing population control. A few positive words from the pope would put the quietus on antiabortion idiocy.

HIGHER EDUCATION AND THE VATICAN
(NOVEMBER 1999)

The National Conference of Catholic Bishops has adopted new guidelines to strengthen the bond between Catholic colleges and the Catholic Church. The guidelines require that newly appointed Catholic college presidents profess the Catholic faith and their personal commitment to the Catholic Church. The guidelines also dictate that the presidents of Catholic colleges take appropriate steps to insure that Catholics constitute a majority of the faculty and the membership of the board of trustees. The guidelines have been submitted to the Vatican for final approval.

For an extensive period, the Vatican has been engaged in a campaign to insure that Catholic colleges are more directly related to the

Catholic Church. In the United States, more than two hundred colleges and universities are considered Catholic institutions even though non-Catholics represent a significant percentage of the faculties and the boards of trustees. These colleges and universities are predominately secular in nature, and the bonds with the Catholic Church are related to the stated objectives of the institution rather than designated legal authority.

The reaction of the leadership in Catholic colleges to these new rules has been mixed and ambivalent. Some academic leaders stress that during the past quarter of a century, Catholic colleges have evolved into essentially secular institutions, and that the new guidelines will have only minimal impact. Other presidents at Catholic colleges are concerned that the new edicts will curtail academic freedom. Since professors who are responsible for teaching theology at these colleges will be required to secure certification from the local bishop that their teachings reflect "authentic Catholic doctrine," there is deep concern that the new guidelines might give credence to the long-term anxiety that professors at Catholic colleges would not then be guaranteed the right of free inquiry.

It is probable that the resolution of these complex issues will be related to sources of college funding rather than theology. If the secular but Catholic-related colleges and universities can flourish with private sources of funding not related to the Catholic Church, the new guidelines may represent only a limited threat to the continuity of the present system.

If the Catholic bishops in the United States can persuade the Vatican that Church doctrine may be vitiated and that secular professors and trustees constitute a danger to the influence of the Catholic Church, many Catholic colleges may be in jeopardy.

If the Catholic Church wants to qualify for a share of the public largesse through the voucher system applied to the parochial schools, the bishops should repudiate the latest effort to curtail the presence of non-Catholics in teaching and policy-making roles at the Catholic-oriented colleges.

AIDS AND CATHOLIC PRIESTS
(FEBRUARY 2000)

In the United States, according to a news report, the incidence of AIDS among Catholic priests is three times greater than that of the general population.

THE SAINTS AND JOHN PAUL II
(MAY 2000)

In his twenty-two years as pope, John Paul II has bestowed 296 canonizations. His predecessor, Paul VI, granted 62 in a period of fifteen years. In third place is Pius IX who performed the deed 52 times in thirty-two years. Since 1740, the total number of canonizations including John Paul II's 296, is 562; therefore, the incumbent pope is responsible for more than half of the total in a period of 360 years.

Designation as a saint does not imply that miracles have been performed; however, 296 saints in our generation does stretch credulity.

JESUIT WRITING AND THE VATICAN
(MARCH 2001)

According to the *New York Times*, Fr. Jacques Dupuis, a Jesuit from Belgium, worked for thirty years in India as a Roman Catholic priest. A few years ago, he arrived in Rome to teach theology at the Pontifical Gregorian University. In 1997, he completed a book titled *Toward a Christian Theology of Religious Pluralism*. In September 1998, the leader of the Jesuit order was informed by Cardinal Joseph Ratzinger, director of the Congregation for the Doctrine of the Faith in the Vatican, that Father Dupuis's book was being investigated.

Subsequently, Father Dupuis received twelve pages of questions, and he sent two hundred pages in response. After seven months of further review, he was notified that his answers were not "satisfactory." He responded once again with sixty more pages answering twelve pages of additional questions.

On September 4, 2000, Father Dupuis was summoned by Cardinal Ratzinger. He was requested to sign a fifteen-page "notification," approved by the pope, that cited "grave errors" in his book. On September 5, the Vatican issued a document from Cardinal Ratzinger stating the primacy of the Roman Catholic Church and alleging that other denominations were "deficient." After several cardinals criticized the tenor of the document, Father Dupuis received a revised draft of the September 4 "notification" changing the accusation of "grave errors" to "ambiguities."

Father Dupuis stated that his superiors convinced him that by signing the document he would be able to continue his theological work. In December 2000, he signed the revised notification to which the Vatican appended a codicil obligating him to "abide" by the concerns regarding his work. Father Dupuis is convinced that he was only required to "take the Vatican's concerns into account."

In February 2001, more than two years after the Vatican investigation began, Father Dupuis, aged seventy-seven, was formally rebuked. The rebuke concluded that his writings on religious pluralism that suggested other faiths might lead to salvation, "contained ambiguities" that could lead to "erroneous or harmful positions" regarding Church doctrine.

The document that Father Dupuis signed in December 2000, and the February 2001 rebuke, will allow Father Dupuis to publish his book, but the Vatican's warnings must be incorporated. Father Dupuis hopes to continue with his writing, but it is obvious that the investigation of his manuscript will deter other theologians from alleged doctrinal deviation.

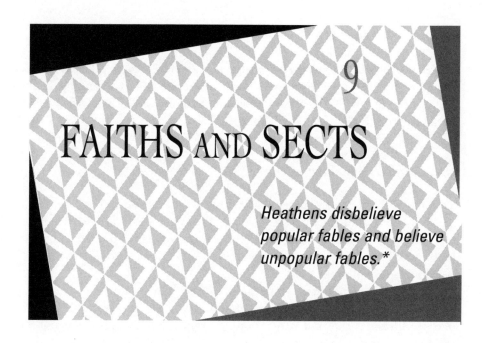

FAITHS AND SECTS

9

*Heathens disbelieve
popular fables and believe
unpopular fables.**

CHRISTIANS AND JEWS

Christianity and the Greeks

During a lifetime of exposure to Christianity (in small, infrequent doses), I had assumed that the elements of the doctrine derived from Jesus and contemporary and subsequent disciples and interpreters. As usual, there is nothing new under the proverbial sun. For example, take a quick glance at the credo of the pre-Christian Greek religion.

Although the ancient Greeks endorsed anthropomorphic deities, limited dogmatism, and minimal enforcement of orthodoxy, Athena appeared by motherless birth from Zeus, and many of the Greek deities have survived as Christian saints. The Greeks believed in life after death and in prayer (which was not considered sufficient per se). There was no creed, no proselytizing, and established heroes could qualify as gods because power was more meaningful than righteousness.

69

To further illustrate the sagacity of the Greek mind, Homer conceived of Heaven on Earth and Plato formulated the Heaven and Hell dichotomy. In the Old and New Testaments, many of the ancient Greek parables were incorporated without attribution.

The Greeks did bear gifts!

Deism and Thomas Jefferson

Thomas Jefferson was a deist. Since the early nineteenth century, few have claimed that distinction. Deists believe that God created the world, but that since that act, he has ignored his creation. The Deists further believe that God can be endorsed on rational grounds without resorting to revelation.

If God can be defined as unknown rather than as "good" (per Mary Baker Eddy and the Christian Scientists), then I am in reasonable proximity to Deism rather than any contemporary religious sect. As usual, I am a few centuries out of step. The essential conundrum remains. God is a figment of the human mind whether the thought process is rational or irrational.

Southern Baptists

In previous years, the Southern Baptist Convention (representing the largest Protestant denomination) has published pamphlets soliciting prayers from Muslims and Jews that only succeeded in antagonizing religious representatives of those faiths. In 1999, the Southern Baptists announced that 30,000 pamphlets would be issued to correspond with the celebration of Divali, a major Hindu festival of lights. The pamphlet alleged that Hindus do not have any concept of sin. If the Southern Baptist Convention continues with this tack, it will be appropriate for them to confront the Catholic Church.

The Role of a Protestant Bishop

The Evangelical Lutheran Church and the Episcopal Church (with a combined following of eight million members) have arranged a form of marriage. The two sects will recognize all members of both groups, and will endorse all of the existing sacraments. They will join hands in missionary and social work endeavors and exchange clergy where circumstances warrant.

This marriage agreement reflects more than thirty years of discussion between the two religious entities; however, the basic tenets of each faith have not been merged. Of greater immediate importance, the office of bishop which is an integral component of the Episcopal Church has not been recognized by the Evangelical Lutheran Church. I would suggest that thirty more years may elapse before that significant conflict is resolved. In the meantime, both groups should concentrate on raising funds for social work. An Episcopal bishop should not be assigned to the task.

The Anglican Communion and Sexual Preference

Traditionally, the Church of England and the Episcopal Church of the United States have tended to dominate the affairs of the worldwide Anglican Communion. The communion includes thirty-eight distinct church groups. Now, Anglican leaders from Southeast Asia, Africa, South America, and the Caribbean are challenging the leadership of the North Americans and the Europeans. The selected battlefield involves the recent decisions of the Episcopal bishops from the developed countries who have ordained noncelibate gay men and lesbians as priests. Archbishops from the developing world are challenging the decisions on the grounds that they do not fall within the traditional boundaries of Christianity and the Church.

In defense of the actions, the bishop of the Episcopal Church in the United States has suggested that the current attacks relate to a mistaken emphasis on "sexuality rather than salvation." He also opines that the concern relates to the historic role of the United States and western Europe as colonial powers and as exporters of Western culture.

In this escalating debate, very little scripture, theology, or religious credo can be detected. Increasingly, the bones of contention emphasize racial, economic, and cultural realities that are debated at the United Nations.

An Episcopal Holiday Service

At 11:00 P.M. on Christmas Eve, we arrived at the Episcopal Church for the holiday service. The "high" Episcopal ritual, featuring innumerable "ups and downs" was dull, formalistic, devoid of substance, and represented the antithesis of the joyous Christmas spirit. The selected parable involved wolves (the venal outside world) that were trying to devour you and me. There was no message other than a carelessly thrown ton of prejudicial verbal bricks. The congregation was bored but dutiful. After the offering was collected, we departed before Jesus was figuratively eaten and drunk.

Who are we to attach the word "pagan" to inoffensive, sustaining, emotionally charged African, Eskimo, and indigenous American rites? Is it not preferable to sing songs of joy praising the gods rather than assembling to drink the blood of Christ and to collect the funds to sustain the process?

The Pennsylvania Amish

In Europe the Amish were a fundamentalist offshoot of the Mennonites. In 1720, they arrived in eastern Pennsylvania. The largest group of descendants resides in the "Pennsylvania Dutch" farm country south of Lancaster.

The towns of Bird-in-Hand and Intercourse are the main Amish shopping marts in the area. North of Route 340, Amish farms dot the landscape in well-kempt profusion. At any time of year the rolling hills are beautiful. The farms are immaculate; the houses and barns are freshly painted and attractive. The denizens of all ages are clean, quiet, well-dressed, and comely, and the customs and dress are quaint.

Unfortunately, behind the picturesque facade, the Amish customs are in jeopardy in an increasingly interdependent world. The dark dress and beards are a throwback to rural customs in Europe two and a half centuries ago rather than to religious precept. Religious beliefs appear to have dictated the absence of churches, telephones, electricity, automobiles, or mechanized farm equipment. The most devastating religious tenet allows Amish children to attend public elementary schools but precludes attendance at public or private high schools.

As an aberration, the Amish will survive for a few generations (until the sustained pressure from the adjoining non-Amish communities intervenes). Parts of the excellent movie *Witness*, featuring Harrison Ford, were filmed in the Amish country of eastern Pennsylvania. With charm and accuracy, it captures the core of the Amish approach to life. At the same time, the movie depicts the increasing relevance of the outside world.

The next Amish generation will be unable to resist the gross temptations of the majority culture that surrounds their temporary Eden. In the meantime, the Amish represent a religious faith that has practical meaning for its adherents.

The Shakers**

In the 1780s, the Shaker village at Canterbury, New Hampshire, was founded. It was the sixth of nineteen Shaker enclaves that were created from Maine to Kentucky. At Canterbury, before the Civil War, three hundred people were resident in one hundred buildings on 4,000 acres. Until recently, Canterbury was one of only two villages with resident Shakers (the two remaining members of the faith are now deceased).

For two centuries, the Shakers devoted their "hands to work and their hearts to God." They practiced racial and gender equality, community ownership of property, celibacy, and pacifism. Since the order survived for two hundred years, celibacy, obviously involved abstinence from marriage rather than sexual intercourse. It is also possible that youthful converts perpetuated the order.

The Shakers represented unique approaches to crafts, furniture, architecture, and the performing arts. Founded in England as an offshoot of the Quakers, they derived their name from ritualistic practices of dancing, whirling, and shaking, which they borrowed from the French. At a time when conventional sects disapproved of dancing, the Shakers choreographed intricate dances as an integral part of their church services. Their farms were exemplary (the Shakers were the first to package seeds), and they were responsible for many inventions including the clothespin. In sustained defiance of the norm, Shaker villages were closed on the Sabbath.

It is understandable that a group that believed and practiced equality, morality, hard work, and peace would have become virtually extinct.

The Church of Jesus Christ of Latter-day Saints

In the summer following my high school graduation, I traveled to Utah to learn more about the Mormon religion and the Mormon people. For several weeks, I lived and pitched peas on a farm near Spanish Fork. As part of my orientation, I read the Book of Mormon, attended Sunday church services, and visited the Mormon-sponsored Brigham Young

University as well as the Mormon Temple in Salt Lake City. Subsequently, I had the pleasure of visiting the Mormon Temple on the island of Oahu in Hawaii, and in several overseas posts I met young Mormon missionaries.

I have deep respect for the attractive, hard-working Mormon people. I have very little respect for the fundamentals of the Mormon religion. Joseph Smith's discovery of the Mormon scripture under a tree in western New York State created a homely North American counterpart for the Bible. The contents have been subjected to even greater scrutiny concerning authenticity than the scriptures of other religious sects.

The moral code of the Mormon religion is exemplary, and the allegations of racial prejudice and polygamy are outdated and overstated. The young missionaries are engaged in "good works" in the lesser-developed world, and the Mormon temples are beautiful with their clean straight lines and lovely gardens.

I was particularly impressed by the Latter-day Saints "testimony" at monthly church meetings. Like the Friends, the Mormons wait for inspiration, while attending church, and the role of church officialdom is minuscule. Parishioners rise to describe the real issues that impact on their lives and solicit the guidance and solace of their peers.

The most damaging trait of the Mormons is not the lack of facts related to the scriptures but the certitude of its members. In that regard, the Mormons resemble every other Christian sect with which I am familiar (with the possible exception of the Friends).

The Limited "Golden Rule"

"Love they neighbor as thyself." This basic credo of the Jewish faith, and as expressed in variable forms by many religions, ignores the innate selfishness of most human beings. Love of self does not normally encompass consideration or pathos. Self-love is related to ego, competitiveness, and self-advancement. These qualities convey the antithesis of love.

Most of the major religions inculcate some version of the "Golden Rule"; however, the sentiment reflects the least common denominator in social interaction. If I am raised in a setting in which child abuse and the absence of love prevail, it is unlikely that I will expect exemplary behavior from the person next door.

Religion fails when it does not require a higher standard of personal behavior than that expected from a neighbor or even from yourself. Looking around us, it is evident that most people act as their neighbors act and behave as their progenitors.

Let us be honest and amend this rule. Fewer people every year pay lip service to the concept, and the anachronistic religious dogma it represents should be replaced with a meaningful social ethic. The ethic, based on statutory not natural law, should be enforced in the home, and in the community, and should not be relegated to the obscurity of the church and the synagogue.

As a starter, may I suggest: Treat your neighbor as your neighbor should have been taught to treat you.

Kosher Food

Many years ago, El Al Airlines lost its kosher catering license because Chief Sephardic Rabbi Ovadia Yosek decreed that El Al was preparing food on the Sabbath and was not keeping separate pans for milk and meat dishes. In a successful effort to regain the license, El Al executives stated that the catering subsidiary strictly observed the religious law and that they required a rabbi to supervise the kitchens. Additional concessions were extracted. The airline agreed to increase the number of kitchen supervisors, and it was stipulated that dirty pots were to be cleaned in the kosher manner.

Up to this point, I understood the rationale of the chief sephardic rabbi; however, El Al also consented to surrender the keys to its kitchens on the Sabbath. Rabbi Yosel had sufficient faith to prepare the meals according to religious rules, but his limited faith in humanity denied the cooks access to the kitchen.

HINDUS, BUDDHISTS, AND MUSLIMS

Hindu Scripture

The Bhagavad Gita (the "Song of God") is the most influential Hindu religious text. It was written in the first or second century A.D., and it is rather short in the genre of religious treatises (700 Sanskrit verses in eighteen chapters).

The "Song of God" depicts a battle in which our hero, Krishna, is the plaintiff for self-discipline. He opines that there are three distinct disciplines that secure release from transmigration (incarnation of the transfer of a soul into another body following death). Since release from transmigration is the basic objective of life, the three disciplines that lead to release are critical.

The first is the discipline of action. Krishna informs us that action per se does not preclude release, but that selfish motivations are the culprit. This is distinct from Buddhists, and some Hindus, who suggest that abstention from action is a sine qua non for release from reincarnation. This prohibition against action is manifested in the doctrine of *Ahimsa*, "nonviolence," which motivated Mahatma Gandhi's policy of nonviolent protest and also the doctrine that prevents a believer from harming any living thing.

In the English translation of the Bhagavad Gita, the discipline of action is translated as "doing your duty without attainment." If attainment means "without hope of credit," the saying is meaningful. If "attainment" is translated as "accomplishment" or "completion," the implication is obtuse. I believe that the quest for attainment must incorporate a concept of duty; therefore, I would tend to side with Krishna.

The second discipline cited by Krishna provides yogic release and closely resembles Ahimsa. There are innumerable yoga applications and schools of thought that are based on this self-discipline.

The final discipline enunciated by Krishna requires a superior devotion to God. The rules to reflect that devotion are virtually infinite.

Clearly, the three disciplines attempt to reconcile variable points of view. Admirable behavior does not guarantee admission to Heaven. Unless the specific Hindu laws are followed with precision, good behavior will not suffice.

To illustrate further Krishna's desire to reconcile, it is alleged that the Bhagavad Gita constitutes justification for the caste system, while, at the same time, its precepts continue to shape the attitudes, values, and the search for inner-peace of modern Hindus.

In the Hindu religion, terror rather than love is generally associated with God. Again, it is difficult to reconcile the fear of God's terror with the objective of inner-peace. If inner-peace rather than service to humankind is the ultimate goal, it is also difficult to perceive of Hinduism as anything more than an egocentric quest for a release from transmigration.

With this essay, my purpose is to illustrate the complexities and incongruities of non-Christian religions. When Christians disparage other religions because they are "simplistic," or lacking a credo, felonies are being compounded.

A Kali Temple

A midday visit to a Calcutta Kali (Goddess of Death) Temple was a shattering experience. Hundreds of maimed paupers inundated the premises. They were anticipating free meals distributed by the Hindu staff. Goats were being slaughtered to gain points with the deity. Beggars inside and outside the temple were omnipresent. The filth was indescribable. The odors were oppressive. The crunch of humanity was frightening.

There was no discipline, no control, no ostensible sign of authority. There was no indication that Kali religious practices mean anything more than a sanction to kill goats, to pollute, and to sponsor a limited feeding program for a few severely handicapped paupers who reside on the sidewalks surrounding the temple.

Christianity may be irrelevant; the Muslims may preach bellicosity; but there is not a shred of evidence to suggest that the Kali Hindu Temple in Calcutta has any long-term substantive meaning for its adherents.

Buddhism and Billy Graham

Billy Graham said that you "can't be Buddhist and Christian at the same time." For those who are unaware of either religion, they might qualify for both without being aware of their good fortune. For those who recognize the existence of both religions, they could cheat a bit by qualifying for both, affiliating with both, and failing to inform the religious authorities.

What the Reverend Billy Graham really meant was that his interpretation of Christianity will not provide a sanctuary for avowed Buddhists. If God, any god, really cared about this distinction, neither religion would merit attention. If a person believes that a devotee cannot be a Christian and a Buddhist simultaneously, he or she does not warrant the designation as a Christian (or a Buddhist). If the Buddhists concur with Dr. Graham's evaluation, which they probably do, we have identified another disease that affects organized religion.

God would never punish a Christian for believing in the tenets of another religion. Why would a god or the gods punish a believer for interpreting his, her, or their positive impact in different ways? Dr. Graham should be commanded by God to live abroad for several years.

The Taliban and the Standing Buddhas

Afghanistan is located in a part of Asia where religions have coexisted for many centuries (Buddhism, Hinduism, and the late arrival, Islam). Before Islam's advent, Afghanistan became the situs of a great Buddhist monastic center. The center generated new religious concepts and created a new religious art that included the world's largest rock carvings of the standing Buddha. The two statues, which probably dated from the seventh century, were 175 feet and 120 feet tall. They were carved into the solid rock on a mountainside in Bamiyan which is located ninety miles west of the Afghan capital of Kabul. The two standing figures are considered to be the finest examples of early Buddhist art.

In recent years, the smaller standing statue was badly damaged by rocket fire during the Afghan-Soviet War. The larger statue was relatively intact, but the head was darkened as the result of tires that were placed around its neck and burned.

Eight centuries ago, the great Buddhas of Bamiyan survived the cannon fire of Genghis Khan, but all previous efforts to desecrate the icons were meaningless compared to the recent Taliban efforts.

The Taliban movement, which annexed 95 percent of Afghanistan through acts of war, endorses a strict interpretation of Islam that requires women to wear the head-to-toe Burqa sheathing, forbids them to work outside the home, and refuses to provide education for girls. Men must wear beards. If they trim their beards, they are incarcerated. Men are also required to pray in the Mosque.

In late February 2001, Mullah Muhammed Olmar, the Taliban's supreme leader, proclaimed the destruction of all statues that "have been Gods of the infidels." At the same time, Taliban military leaders admitted that all non-Islam religious artifacts were being systematically destroyed with hand tools and explosives. It was also revealed that the "heads and legs of the Buddha statues in Bamiyan had been obliterated." The Taliban minister of information and culture stated: "Our soldiers are working hard to demolish the remaining parts. . . . It is easier to destroy than to build."

The United Nations led a belated effort to rescind the decision to destroy the statues, but the UNESCO director agreed that the attempt was hopelessly tardy and that the threat was a "mindless aggression to a part of the conscience, history, and identity of mankind." Pakistan, the Taliban's closest ally, joined the endeavor to reverse the decision. Pakistan's foreign minister stated that "respect for other religions and for their beliefs is enjoined upon Muslims." In Egypt, the most senior Muslim cleric said that retention of the standing statues "would not have any impact on Muslims' beliefs" and is not forbidden by Islam.

Iran's foreign ministry issued a statement blaming the "rigid-minded Taliban" and suggested that "the destruction of the statues has cast doubt on the comprehensive views offered by the Islamic ideology." The leader of UNESCO's Arab group described the action as "savage." The director of the Metropolitan Museum of Art in New York City informed the secretary-general of the United Nations that the museum would pay the costs of removing the statues from Afghanistan. Based on precedent, such a feat would be virtually impossible. Since the proposal was not endorsed by senior U.S. government officials, the offer was ignored by the Taliban.

The current plight of the Afghan people is deplorable. Famines have become endemic. Since the fall of 2000, more than 700,000 Afghan people have fled from their homes. In total, more than one million became refugees. These figures predate the 2001 war in which the Taliban government was removed.

In searching for a Taliban rationale for the mayhem, it has been suggested that the elimination of Afghanistan's pre-Islamic heritage may be related to the sanctions that were imposed unanimously by the United Nations in January 2000. A coalition composed of the United States, China, and Russia provided the leadership at the United Nations that led to the sanctions. The sanctions were retaliation for Afghanistan's failure to surrender Saudi terrorist leader, Osmana bin Laden. Before the recent war, the Taliban stated that other nations are "not kind to Afghanistan."

In refutation of this explanation, the Taliban banned the growing of poppies, which are required to prepare heroin. Afghanistan is the largest world producer, and the income from the sales of the product is its largest revenue source.

Independent of the rationale, and in spite of unanimous external opposition, including Buddhist leaders from several countries, the destruction of the statues went ahead as planned.

In 1992, Hindu militants in India destroyed the Muslim Mosque at Ayodhya, but the unanimous negative reaction to the Bamiyan devastation has been unprecedented. It is not reassuring that the universal response to the famine imposed upon hundreds of thousands of Afghan refugees has not been comparable.

A few comparative religion scholars have suggested that the Islamic religion is extroverted, and that the theology of Islam does not convey a sense of guilt. The overwhelming condemnation of the Taliban acts by Islamic world leaders has vitiated this argument.

The Koran states: "I do not serve what you worship; nor do you serve what I worship. You have your own religion, and I have mine." Unfortunately, most religious groups, and factions spawned by these groups, tend to absorb the cultural, political, national, and societal values of the area where the congregation resides. Adherents of religious doctrine do not exist in a vacuum. Faith-based dogma does not imply rectitude.

Sharia

In late 1983, President Nemieri, a career military officer who assumed power in the Sudan, transformed a moderately progressive nation into a controlled Muslim state by an arbitrary, unilateral edict. At that time, "Sharia," the Swahili and Arabic term for "law," was imposed upon an affable, apolitical, uncomplicated populace. "Sharia" incorporates into a rule of law an extensive number of Islamically inspired prohibitions that handicap normal human behavior. For example, the purchase, possession, use, and sale of alcoholic beverages are proscribed. Violators are subject to jail sentences and flogging.

Legal sages have suggested that hard cases make bad law. The corollary is also true. Bad law begets hard cases.

A Finnish businessman arrived at Khartoum Airport with the intention of engaging in normal commercial transactions. Reflecting Finnish practice, his luggage included three bottles of whiskey to present to his regular clients in the Sudan. The customs authorities inquired whether the Finnish traveler had any intoxicating beverages in his possession. Reflecting another Finnish practice, a unique proclivity for honesty, the weary traveler extracted the three bottles from his luggage, placed them on the counter, and inquired about the duty to be assessed.

Naivete, thy name is Finn! Our contemporary "teller of no lies" was arrested, placed in a jail cell, and informed that his sentence would be ninety days and thirty lashes. Since Finland was not represented in the Khartoum version of the Corps Diplomatique, the prisoner remained in his "dry" cell for a few days before the minister of foreign affairs convinced the president of Sudan that their putative reputation as a compassionate neighbor in the world community might be in jeopardy.

I am doubtful that our Finnish entrepreneur will return to the land of broken profit-oriented dreams or that Finnish tourism will become a prominent source of Sudanese foreign exchange.

In the cited case, quaint little Muslim idiosyncracies could have been equally well served by confiscating the offensive elixir and sending the Finn to his clients without bearing gifts.

In the capital city, the Sudanese government has erected a monument, at a prominent traffic circle, commemorating the government's decision to relegate existing liquor supplies to the bottom of the Nile. In contrast to the impact of a historic Boston jettisoning party, I doubt that any cause was served other than the sense of well-being of the agnostic Nile perch.

Without exception, the remarkably attractive, articulate, educated, caring Sudanese people whom I met condemned the "Sharia" edicts. They asserted that unless the Sharia proscriptions were repealed, the Sudan would continue to lose credibility, investment potential, and the revenue from tourism and other foreign exchange sources. Of greater importance, the security forces charged with enforcing the law created a "big brother" environment that was demeaning and enervating.

For the diplomatic corps in Khartoum, "Sharia" has presented major survival problems. Can you imagine attending seventy-five national day celebrations per year without the benefit of something stronger than water from the Nile?

When "Sharia" was promulgated, the bans did not extend to three Sudanese states (provinces) that are African (black), Christian, and/or Animist, as well as being impoverished and ignored by the Muslim-Arab controlled central government. The rationale for the exclusion illustrates that the Sudanese government was capable of turning a pragmatic Muslim cheek.

The Muslim Commitment

Because of its religous preoccupation, fervor, demanding regimen, and disdain for competition, Islam is frightening. At the same time, I admire the architecture, the people's dedication, their Hadj commitment, and the openness of the Mosque environment.

The inner-sanctum of the mosque is inaccessible to heathens and to women; however, the peripheral grounds offer a meaningful view of the unhurried, clean, simple, immense, and colorful architecture and the utilitarian applications. The typical mosque seems to reach to the believer rather than to heaven, and it appears to speak to the outside world. In contrast, the "busy," complex, introspective, dark, intimidating architecture of the stereotypic Christian edifice speaks only to itself.

In the outer-sanctum, which includes the school, library, and prayer rooms of a mosque, people live, children play, and adults rest. The scene approximates the way of life on the adjoining streets. In the Christian counterpart, the exterior and interior areas (with the exception of Sunday School space) are forbidding, arcane, lifeless, and deliberately devoid of the real world outside.

The hold of Islam on the devotee is commanding, impressive, and difficult to emulate. With loudspeakers on every minaret broadcasting sermons at least twice per day, reminding the faithful of their servitude, and male prostrated votaries openly declaring their faith by facing Mecca, the overt promotional campaign is unprecedented.

I am convinced that Islam will figure prominently in the next world war. The infidel, in all flavors, will have difficulty combining diverse beliefs and animosities to combat an oppressive religion that captures the daily commitment of the believer and pinpoints the enemy to all those who are not Muslim.

A Projected Muslim War

More than forty years ago, I suggested to my spouse and stated in my journal that the next major war would feature the Muslim world versus the non-Muslim world. The Vietnam War intervened, but it did not involve most of the major powers, and the level of effort was relatively restrained.

It was my thesis then, and now, that the Muslim War would not be fought via conventional means. Terrorism, and provoking civil unrest, would predominate until the evolution in weaponry would allow small Muslim nations to threaten major Western, non-Muslim countries.

With chemical and biological weapons development, the time for escalated warfare is approaching. Terrorism has proven its efficacy, and it would be idiotic, at this juncture, for violence-supporting Muslim factions and/or nations to risk losing their current advantageous position. If Muslim groups continue to manifest cleverness, and to shun a premature major strike, nuclear weapons may become irrelevant. In the meantime, I am not cognizant of any concerted effort to bridge the growing gap between Muslim and non-Muslim interests.

As long as the West, which professes Christianity, maintains superior weaponry, the Muslim world will not risk a fundamental confrontation. If several Muslim nations stockpile nuclear bombs and biological weapons, a war could begin.

In Iraq, Saddam Hussein discharged an essential leadership role in testing the non-Muslim (read the United States and Great Britain) response to increased provocation. It is probable that other Muslim nations will continue to test the commitment of the infidels.

10

RELIGION AND SOCIETY

When dictionaries rather than Bibles are placed in hotel rooms, Civilization may survive.*

RELIGIOUS EXCESS

In Western democracies the tolerance for religious excess appears to be unlimited. The First Amendment insures freedom for a legion of eccentrics to broadcast bizarre versions of limited truth, or outright prevarication, regarding our interpretation of the unknown.

In the West, a panoply of psychotics, misfits, entrepreneurs, and preachers (ordained and otherwise) utilize the natural greed of the media to expand the less than plausible explanations of the inexplicable. The citizenry listens, reads, and smiles, even when the "Moonies" attract the progeny of the wealthy (the Reverend Moon stated that there is no freedom of religion in the United States because the IRS is investigating his failure to pay income tax). We tend to accept the results as innocuous, aberrational behavior.

The threshold of tolerance for religious idiocy ceases when a public figure, or a private figure with public clout, transcends paying lip service to God's will. For example, if a business leader were to pray publicly that God will improve the Dow-Jones index; a former secretary of the interior were to allege that public ownership of the national parks is irrelevant because God will resolve the issue through immediate intervention; a political candidate were to aver that he or she will win an election because of personal support from the almighty, or a sports announcer were to suggest that God looks approvingly at baseball rather than stock-car racing, public support might wane.

On the other hand, the line is fine. The harmless incantation of the Beatitudes, the Lord's Prayer, or the Golden Rule; the inserting of "under God" in the pledge of allegiance to the flag; the making of the sign of the cross to ensure that your foul shot will be successful, or delivering a halftime plea for divine intrusion to insure victory, will not breach the threshold of tolerance.

Religious practice, as with most social realities, constitutes a facade which reassures us that contemporary society is civilized. For most of us, even the most devout religious practice does not affect the quality, affluence, or security of our lives.

INVASIVE RELIGION

For religious zealots (a few of the meek also seem to endorse the practice), engaging in war appears to be more acceptable than "turning the other cheek." The Ten Commandants do not seem to preclude waging nefarious forms of warfare in order to extend the protection of "our" religion to those who do not believe or to those who believe in an improper manner. In addition, even if "our" religion is the same as "yours," we may wage war if your political or economic credo varies from "ours." (World War II is a pertinent example.)

Whatever the rationale, religious beliefs have seldom inhibited those who would like to extend those beliefs to others. In recent centuries, religious missionaries from the developed world, with the power of the modern state behind them, as well as the power of religious certitude, have concentrated on a subtle but effective mode of persuasion. With the Christian version of the Bible in hand, they have attempted to convert "others" to the joys of their unique sect within Christianity. Overt weapons of war have seldom been utilized, but the missionary spirit is expressed within the cocoon of power and righteousness.

In the history of Christianity, the invasive form of religious conversion has been more typical than open warfare, but the results are more lasting. For example, Protestant invasive tactics were employed with the Native American population during the nineteenth-century expansion of the white man's "manifest destiny" doctrine to the Pacific Ocean. The Spanish conquistadores and church representatives relied upon an invasive approach in providing the horse, the gun, and Catholicism for the "pagan" owners of the land in the Western Hemisphere.

The invasive nature of religion has not been confined to Christianity. Shintoism begot Pearl Harbor. The Muslim Sunni and Shiite sects have been known to bash each other with the weapons of war. The Hindus and the Muslims have decimated thousands in India and Pakistan. Even the pacifist Buddhists have been known to raise a hand in anger against a foreign religious movement.

The not so devious gravamen of this argument is that religious restraints on violence and oppression are seldom effective when push comes to shove on the battlefield of self-interest. It is understandable that our ancient forefathers carried staves. They were needed as weapons against the infidel as well as for balance in herding sheep.

FASTING AND THE BOMB

The *New York Times* reports that Mr. Bill Bright of the Campus Crusade for Christ arose from his knees after prayer and said to his wife: "Fasting and prayer is the atomic bomb or the hydrogen bomb of all the Christian disciplines." Ignoring the destructive potential of the hydrogen bomb, I still believe that Mr. Bright is not so, and that he missed the mark.

Following the revelation that he transmitted to his spouse, Mr. Bright illuminated the world by requesting two million fasters in response to his appeal. In the Bible, fasting was depicted as a private manifestation of faith. It would appear that Mr. Bright is convinced that hungry people, in the millions, may have some detonating (oops) impact on the society in which we live. In the same time period, a church worker in Birmingham, Alabama, followed Mr. Bright by issuing the edifying statement: "I wish we devoured God like we devour our food."

Mr. Bright and his colleague in Birmingham must get their acts together. Christian believers cannot have it both ways. Either we should be encouraged to eat or not to eat. In attempting to reconcile the bombastic (there I go again) tirades of our religious heroes from the Campus Crusade and from Birmingham, a significant stretch of faith is required.

Before these men are finished, the big bang theory will represent another Christian discipline. To fast or to eat, that is the combustion.

GOLF AND THE LAST SUPPER

The *New York Times* also reports that Msgr. Louis-Marie Bille is president of the French Bishops' Conference and of "Beliefs and Liberties," which was created by the bishops' conference to bring suit against corporations for advertisements that are considered offensive to the Catholic Church in France.

"Beliefs and Liberties" is exercising its charter by suing Volkswagen of France, and its advertising agency, for four different posters that allegedly mock the scriptures. The most offensive poster, for which "Beliefs and Liberties" is demanding $400,000 in damages, is a parody of the "Last Supper." Emulating Leonardo da Vinci's painting, the ad depicts a group of men in modern attire assembled at a dining table in roughly the same alignment as the disciples in da Vinci's historic work. The man in the center of the table, says: "My friends, let us rejoice because a new Golf is born" (Golf is a Volkswagen species in France).

Msgr. Bernard Lagoutte, secretary-general of the French Bishops' Conference, suggests that the poster per se is not blasphemous; however, "it ridicules a religious image . . . and mockery is a corrosive-like rust that gradually erodes everything." Monsignor Lagoutte also argues that sex in advertising "does not work anymore," and that Christians have become the target (since Muslims retaliate and Jews are guaranteed safe passage because of the Holocaust).

Reflecting the clout of the Catholic Church in France, Volkswagen has terminated the use of religious images in advertising and cancelled the "Last Supper" posters. No further reference to the episode has appeared in the media.

Clearly, the Catholic Church in France, and in several other jurisdictions, lacks "a funny bone." If the response to the advertisements had been "light and easy," Golfs would have been sold and a few more citizens might have heard of the "Last Supper." If an artist's painting depicting an alleged religious event, e.g., the "Last Supper," is acceptable even though it may be factually incorrect, a corporate tongue-in-cheek reference to the same painting should fall within the definition of free speech or at least fair game. In an age when owners consider their vehicles sacrosanct, it is hard to believe that "mockery" would be recognized or that any form of advertising would fail to sell automobiles.

RELIGION AND LONGEVITY

A study by the National Science Foundation suggests that people who attend weekly religious services may live longer (up to seven years) than those who abstain. Immediately, representatives of various religious sects allege that there is a direct link between faith and good health.

If the initial findings are corroborated, the rationale is clear: the magic of a longer life is related to social support services rather than faith. Any social group provides a base for reassurance and a corresponding reduction of stress. In addition, those who attend church are generally less addicted to alcohol and tobacco (related to peer pressure). In any social group, in times of need, friends provide support. The bonding associated with a social group reduces externally stimulated tension. A survey of a garden club, a Boy Scout troop (if the scouts remain in uniform for a lifetime), or a weekly gathering of avowed atheists would probably produce comparable results.

Religion does not represent an opiate, per Lenin, but only a social diversion that reduces stress and creates explosive schisms. In the absence of definitive proof, which will never surface (or descend), nonbelievers will continue to remain silent while believers continue to use the religious and social pulpits with alacrity. The rest of us would prefer something more palatable that will attempt to put religious belief and practice in perspective.

As a college friend advised: "Why do you worry about religion? I am a Catholic. My beliefs are prepared for me and accepted by me in that form. As a result, I have time to devote to other things which I might be able to control." I still believe that my friend is copping out. I also believe that the National Science Foundation should concentrate on longevity in a Garden Club and in a Boy Scout troop.

THE HOLY DAYS OR THE HOLIDAYS

Most of the Christian holidays are based upon pagan rituals that predated Christ for many centuries. Other holy days bear little relationship to Christian scripture.

◈ Good Friday was formerly known as "Great Friday." It is still designated as "Great" in the Eastern Orthodox Church. Whether "Good" or "Great," it designates the day on which Christ was crucified.

◈ On Easter, Christ was resurrected. He left the tomb and walked upon Earth. The specific date when Easter is celebrated depends upon the position of the Moon, stars, etc.

◈ On various occasions, for thirty-nine days, Christ appeared to the disciples. On the fortieth day after Easter—the date varies with the status of the Moon—"Holy Thursday" or Ascension is celebrated. On that date, Christ rose to the Heavens.

◈ Ten days later, on Pentecost, the "Holy Spirit" descended to Earth to imbue the disciples.

The Meaning of Christmas

Until the nineteenth century, the impact of the laws of the Puritans outlawed the celebration of Christmas. The Puritans considered the traditional European Christmas customs (including carols, decorated trees, and the exchange of presents) as pagan practices. If Christmas were observed as a holiday, Commonwealth citizens were subject to punitive action including fines or jail.

In New England, in 1856, Christmas was endorsed as a holiday in the commonwealth of Massachusetts. The Puritan ethic deprecated the random selection of the date for the birth of Christ as well as the frivolity and antireligious nature of the holiday. In Europe, based upon historic pagan rites associated with the winter solstice, the Christmas holiday emerged. In the fourth century A.D., December 25 was selected as the date of the birth of Christ, and the Christian holiday gradually evolved.

A Personal Christmas

For many years, my wife and I acquired Christmas tree ornaments from antique shops in New York City and from emporia where we resided overseas. The remarkable artistry with ancient glass is distinctive and conveys the meaning of Christmas in an unparalleled manner. During their formative years, our children made Christmas tree ornaments, many of which have survived. In addition, silver ornaments, which we purchased for a score of years, provided depth for the more colorful and traditional bells, balls, and Santas.

As the tree was denuded, and the ornaments were carefully stored for another year, it was fun to reminisce about places seen and people met. In contemporary society, it is difficult to allocate time for remembering the moments along the way. The rituals of Christmas afford that opportunity.

The trinkets gathered during a lifetime are relegated to a drawer or a closet or banished to the attic. Efforts are seldom made to enjoy these alleged treasures. The joys of Christmas provide an appropriate forum to compare notes, take stock, share memories, and count your blessings.

Christmas: United States and Europe

At a local church in New England, we attended the children's rendition of the Christmas story. Young teenagers, who were old enough to learn lines, were poorly prepared and inadequately motivated. In Europe, children of comparable age would have staged a sterling performance.

We drove to a neighboring town to observe the Christmas lights. After experiencing the lovely holiday lights in major and minor cities throughout Europe, the local version was a great disappointment.

I am convinced that Americans are only minimally interested in holiday public decorations. Most spending is personal, and public funds are seldom expended for festive, attractive, varied, or creative displays on city streets (the White House Christmas tree and the Rockefeller Center decorations are notable exceptions).

A Bavarian Christmas

During the holiday season, the conservative traits in the Bavarian character are counterbalanced by the captivating customs associated with the Christmas season. Every display is prepared with consummate skill. Every carol is sung with feeling, precision, and expertise. Every colored light is hung with a paradigm in mind, and every artifact reflecting the Christmas motif is created with esthetic awareness and attention to detail.

In contrast to the United States, where the spirit of Christmas appears to be confined to thirty minutes on Christmas Eve, in Bavaria, the entire month of December features a daily exercise in human warmth, including noncommercial smiles from shopkeepers. The pace of life decelerates. Although the almighty Deutsch Mark (Euro) reigns supreme, the basic spirit of Christmas shines through the miasma of the marketplace. If there is a Santa Claus, he or she must spend a bit of time in Bavaria.

Thanksgiving Day

Thomas Jefferson opposed the concept of Thanksgiving Day. He felt that the U.S. government endorsement of gratitude to the divine compromised the separation of church and state. In the intervening years, the religious character of the holiday has been obfuscated by commercialism and gluttony, which are equally offensive, but Jefferson's wise admonition is no longer relevant.

Thanksgiving Day is now devoted to family, overeating, driving or flying hundreds of miles, and preparing for the pre-Christmas sales that are launched the following day.

There is one lingering doubt. The president's annual Thanksgiving Proclamation stresses our national gratitude to God. That reference should be deleted. Since the proclamation is considered boilerplate, and is seldom read, church-state separation is not in jeopardy; however, next November, I will read the document, carefully paying homage to the memory of Thomas Jefferson. Now that President Franklin Roosevelt is deceased, it should be possible to determine the day of celebration with alacrity.

Working on the Sabbath

It appears that the Sabbath is the only day of the week when the indigenous St. Thomians (residents of St. Thomas in the U.S. Virgin Islands) work. The other days are devoted to coffee and beer breakfasts, playing calypso music at the top decibel level, building churches, and leaving the manual labor to the "Down Islanders" (nonindigenous folk).

House construction is also a Sunday pursuit, including Christmas morning. Most stores are open (the cruise ships, you know). Although many of the most prestigious restaurants are closed, and obviously the banks and government offices enjoy the Sabbath, Sunday is a full working day in this tropical paradise.

Since the Bavarian City Fathers do not allow the cutting of grass on Sunday, residency in the Virgin Islands is a vast improvement.

Hate Days

In Cambodia, May 20, 1997, was initially designated "National Hate Day" to commemorate the birthday of Khmer Rouge leader, Pol Pot. Belatedly, wiser heads prevailed, and the celebration was changed to National Remembrance Day, a euphemism to vent anger regarding the atrocities of Pol Pot. Since Cambodia is a devout Buddhist country, the indiscretions of the Khmer Rouge (e.g., "the Killing Fields") were transcended by the gentle reactions of the religious majority in a release of righteous indignation.

Although "Hate Day" failed to survive, I am intrigued by its broader implications. Holidays should observe the warts as well as the blessings of society. "Tricky Dick" Day would capture the negative feelings of a few survivors who remember the truth, and "Killer Rabbit" Day and "Slick Willy" Day would designate other priceless moments in American presidential history. Hate days could serve scores of religious and ethnic purposes. Outlets for prejudice, confined to harmless parades that would only inconvenience traffic, would serve a salutary purpose.

I realize that my proposal is radical, but it is preferable to hate in an innocuous fashion than to reelect bigots or to perpetrate "hate" crimes.

PHILANTHROPY

When we are relatively poor, we have useful ideas about spending money intelligently for the common good. When we become relatively affluent, we forget the lessons of penury and devote our riches to pursuits geared to enhancing personal prestige rather than improvements in the public weal.

To state this truism in another way, if a person dedicates his life to good works, in the absence of affluence, he is considered a social worker, a liberal, or a quack. If a person who has cut ethical corners through real estate and investments amasses a fortune and assigns partial financial gains to the same charities, he is designated a philanthropist and buildings bear his name.

The charitable instinct without wealth is suspect. Wealth, in whatever form and however obtained, can be partially devoted to charity, and the donor becomes a hero. Life is seldom equitable, but in the United States philanthropy has become a joke. We honor the wrong people for giving grants to charities that represent their own personal ambitions. Two generations ago, the same process produced the major foundations. Today, with more complex federal income tax laws, geared to protect the same genre, philanthropy has motivated the renaming of virtually every new building on virtually every college campus and virtually every museum and hospital.

In the meantime, most of us give a few dollars to save the whales with the recognition that 60 percent of our donation will be expended on the perpetuation of a charitable bureaucracy. If I were wealthy, I would probably invest in membership on a few distinguished public boards of directors to make certain that the obituaries would be favorable. If I sold out to the edifice complex, my commitments to the environment and social welfare would be strained. It might be glorious to test that thesis.

In conclusion, philanthropy has nothing to do with religion and very little to do with charity.

POPULATION CONTROL

As a passing reference, I have suggested frequently that nothing in our contemporary existence has greater meaning than population control. For the past several decades, successive waves of Washington politicians have manifested limited commitment to the cause. I now recognize that the United States will not become a world leader in population-control circles.

Now that I have vented my spleen, I am also aware that I have an obligation to support pragmatic approaches to limiting the size of families. As a nonprofessional, it is tempting to leave that responsibility to the nonprofit groups that have been eminently successful in wasting essential financial resources. On the other hand, as a parent who produced one more progeny than the zero population growth prescription, I have a duty to be creative in another sense.

I propose that governments pay citizens for choosing not to have children by utilizing the same rationale as the national policy that reimburses farmers for not planting crops. If a married couple survives two years of marital bliss without progeny, they will be entitled to a $1,000 stipend or gift certificates at two local restaurants. For four years, the entitlement would be a color television set; six years, a new SUV; and eight years, a free week in Las Vegas.

The variations on this avaricious scheme are exciting. If we are able to control world population growth through the lust for things other than children, our tax dollars might then be refunded rather than dedicating those financial resources to sterilized needles for teenagers.

ABORTION

En route to Four Corners Monument, which designates the intersection of Utah, Colorado, Arizona, and New Mexico, a road sign dictated "Adoption not Abortion" (without attribution).

In opposing abortion, we eliminate one of the fundamental rights of women. Through adoption, we increase societal costs that might also include alternative placement in an orphans' home.

To support abortion, as the road sign implies, grants a license for promiscuity. Would not adoption have the same impact?

The old Burma Shave signs were a decided improvement!

TRAITS FOR A VIABLE SOCIETY

In order for society to function with distinction there are four desirable human traits that must be evident in generous supply: sympathy, fairness, self-control, and a sense of duty. A modicum of intelligence would be useful, but let us not be greedy.

These four traits are not endowed by God or related to Natural Law. Unless intelligence is included, heredity is not a relevant factor. All four traits are related. They are learned in the family, in school, and in the workplace. They can be integrated into the concept of "getting along" with fellow human beings. They represent the sine qua non for a meaningful survival.

Why are these traits in such short supply? Most societies do not gear the reward structure to successful attainment of these attributes.

Sympathy is generally perceived as a weakness. Fairness is for the other guy to practice. Self-control is considered boring, and duty was something attributed to Camelot.

If these traits were taught through example at home and in school, the results might be startling. When the typical popular television sit-com places emphasis on fairness rather than winning, on self-control rather than a "high five," on sympathy rather than sex, and on duty rather than "letting it all hang out," our form of democracy might be worth exporting.

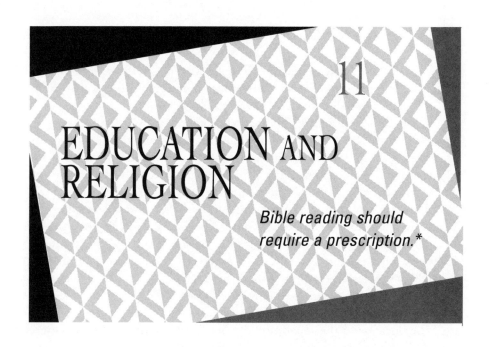

EDUCATION AND RELIGION

*Bible reading should require a prescription.**

THE FOUNDING FATHERS AND RELIGION

In the ancient Athenian city-state it was possible to instill moral values without an underlying religious precept. In a modern democracy it is also feasible to nurture ethical values without the guidance of religious credo.

Since the American Revolution religion has represented a very important societal dimension without becoming a fixture of constitutional law. The Declaration of Independence enshrines the objective that "all men are created equal and endowed by their Creator with certain inalienable rights." The Constitution of the United States was promulgated "in the year of our Lord (1787)." Generally, these commitments have not been translated into legal rights.

In contrast, the Bill of Rights decrees that "Congress shall make no law respecting the establishment of religion or prohibiting the free exercise thereof." This prohibition has established definitive legal rights that are subject to judicial interpretation. Deliberately, the freedom of religion guaranteed by the Bill of Rights was left vague.

97

The United States was not launched as a Christian nation. For example, it is impossible to determine the intent of the Founding Fathers with regard to religion in the public schools.

With the exception of Thomas Jefferson, not one of the pundits involved with the creation of the nation commented specifically on freedom of religion. Jefferson asserted that it was "the purpose of the First Amendment to build a wall of separation between church and state," and his statement is considered the genesis of that doctrine.

Jefferson's dictum had overt impact on the United States Supreme Court, which ruled, among other things, that a vocal reading of a prayer in a public classroom violated the First Amendment. For generations, individual states have attempted to bypass this decision without success. Thomas Jefferson embellished the doctrine by refusing to allow a professorship in theology at the public University of Virginia, which he founded.

The doctrine of the separation of church and state, for which there is no constitutional justification, was not imposed with a nonreligious hand. In 1864, two-cent coins were minted with the phrase "In God We Trust." In subsequent decades, the same phrase was included on other denominations of coinage. In 1956, the phrase became the national motto without provoking a sustained legal outcry.

As a schoolboy, when I recited the Pledge of Allegiance, there was no reference to religion. Without fundamental opposition, in 1954, the United States Congress added the words "under God."

As a Boy Scout, I invoked the oath: "On my honor I will do my best to do my duty to God and my country," and the twelfth and final point of the Scout Law stipulates that "a Scout is reverent" (toward God and in his religious duties).

These minor concessions to religion were not considered infractions of the separation doctrine; however, in 1962, the Supreme Court expressed the view that liberal interpretation of the separation doctrine must be curtailed. Until that year, voluntary prayer in the public schools was allowed. Charting a more restrictive course, the Supreme Court held that school-organized, directed, or sponsored religious activity, vocal classroom prayers, and devotional Bible reading were proscribed in the public schools. Subsequently, the Supreme Court extended the ruling to school-sponsored events external to the classroom and to revising the curriculum to reflect the tenets of any faith. Student religious clubs and silent prayer are allowed; however, it has been established that because the practice will lead to sectarian favoritism or emphasis, the public schools may not promote religion in general terms.

Local and state governments and organizations continue to introduce proposals that would endorse religious practices in the public schools and breach the doctrine of church-state separation.

When the Harvard Medical School added a curricular requirement that all psychiatry majors must complete a course in spirituality, there was great excitement in the religious fundamentalist camp. Conveniently, they forgot that Harvard is a private institution, and that the Harvard decision was based on the needs of psychiatric patients rather than vitiating the separation of church and state.

National neutrality with regard to religion should not be equated with substantive opposition. Society, not the neutrality of the federal government with regard to religion, increased the incidence of teenage crime and the number of unwed mothers. In the unique and generally successful brand of democracy practiced in the United States, national neutrality in the field of religion has worked and is working. Before endorsing religious training and organized prayer in the public schools, religious conservatives should evaluate the alternative.

A national government that endorsed religion would be forced to assume a leadership role in the battle of sects.

Secular Humanism

In 1985, Sen. Orrin Hatch of Utah introduced a bill to prevent the teaching of "secular humanism" in the public schools. Without debate, or even defining the term, the Senate and the House of Representatives enacted the legislation. It was subsequently endorsed by the Reagan White House. The author of "benign neglect," Sen. Daniel Patrick Moynihan of New York State, approved the measure because it was "innocuous."

Under the terms of the legislation, schools that are subject to desegregation in local districts will not benefit from federal funding unless they comply with the "secular humanism" edict.

Several years were required to formulate the guidelines and regulations through the U.S. Department of Education. The federal regulations also failed to define the term; therefore, a unique legislative responsibility was ignored.

What did Senator Hatch have in mind? Based on collateral discussion, it is clear that public school children, in schools that enjoy federal support, would not be exposed to Darwin, birth control, abortion, sex education, or other "exotic" themes. In history courses, the reality of the unequal distribution of wealth would probably be disregarded. In social studies, emphasis would be placed on the role of religion in the family. In civics, the absence of dissent would be equated with patriotism. In all public school classes, a simplistic view of God would be honored to the exclusion of comparative religion or the fetters of the Christian religion. In economics, liberal and socialist options would be rejected, and in general science, ecology and conservation would be replaced by endorsement of acid rain and land exploitation.

A BIBLE COURSE IN HIGH SCHOOL

In the current saga of the fundamentalist religious "right," it is frightening to consider the impact of the National Council for Bible Curriculum. The council has been remarkably successful in securing approval for teaching the Bible in the public school curricula of twenty-two states.

In 1997, in North Carolina, with the generous assistance of the active council, twenty school districts offered a Bible course. The actual course content was provided by the National Council. In a single district in North Carolina, with a total of 11,000 eligible students, four hundred enrolled in the elective course.

In the 1960s, the "Bible Course" issues were resolved by the U.S. Supreme Court. It is patently clear that the Bible course approach now being implemented would not withstand a constitutional challenge. To reduce the potential of a direct confrontation on constitutional grounds, the National Council claims that the course is being taught as history and that moral issues are not incorporated. If religions other than Christianity were embraced in the course, the argument might merit attention.

Unless there is a timely church-state separation legal challenge, the virus will spread. As the religious right gains power through subtle changes such as the Bible course at the secondary school level, essential freedoms may become endangered.

THE KANSAS SCHOOLS AND EVOLUTION

More than three-quarters of a century ago, noted trial lawyer Clarence Darrow vindicated the teaching of evolution in the public schools. Unfortunately, the *Scopes* trial did not terminate the debate.

In 1987, the U.S. Supreme Court supported the result of the *Scopes* trial by holding that the science of creation was only religion in wolf's clothing and that the teaching of that discipline was prohibited by the Constitution. Both the initial Bush administration and the Clinton administration have endorsed the need for national guidelines that pinpoint the requirement of evolutionary teaching in the science curriculum.

During the past decade, the national guidelines have triggered an adverse reaction to alleged federal interference in local and state rights in the field of public education. They have used the teaching of evolution as the cornerstone of their complaint. Of the fourteen states involved, only Nebraska, Illinois, Alabama, and Kansas have taken action. In Nebraska, warnings have been issued to the school system, without sanctions, regarding the teaching of evolution. In Illinois, evolution is considered "a controversial issue." In Alabama, biology and geology textbooks must stipulate that evolution is "theory, not fact."

In Kansas, the board of education has taken definitive action in repudiating the doctrine of evolution. In August 1999, the state board of education (in a six-to-four vote that reflected conservative-moderate positions) expressed displeasure with national guidelines and struck evolution from the high school curricula in science.

The Kansas decision represents a sea change in opposition to evolution. Since national opinion polls reported in the *New York Times* have discovered that only 10 percent of the American people believe that life on Earth evolved without the benefit of divine intervention, the gap in understanding has presented a field day for modern "creationists." Rather than relying upon the old arguments about monkeys, they have alleged that "evolution is not science," and that evolution is pure fiction because it has not been "observed" in action. Modern "creationists" have convinced the overwhelming majority that an intelligent power rather than mere random choice has produced *Homo sapiens*.

The Kansas Board of Education ruling is the latest episode in a concerted effort by religious fundamentalists to restrict, revise, or eliminate the teaching of evolution in the public schools. Modern students may inherit the blarney as well as the wind.

(In late 2000, based on public pressure, the Kansas Board of Education reversed its ruling. Now, both evolution and creationism can be taught in the Kansas high school curriculum.)

THE TEN COMMANDMENTS AND STEVE FORBES

In September 1999, at a high school in Des Moines, Iowa, Steve Forbes (editor of *Forbes* magazine and Republican presidential candidate) informed his audience that the Ten Commandments should be displayed in American schools because they represent "the basis of this civilization. The Koran is not the basis of this civilization; the Ten Commandments are. If you went to, say, a country that has the Muslim religion, and you go to a school, you might expect to see the Koran there, you wouldn't be surprised. It's part of their culture. It's the same thing here." This comment by Mr. Forbes is jingoistic and misleading, but he had the right to state it.

The Ten Commandments are not the basis of the American culture. Democracy is the basis, and freedom of religion is one of the cornerstones of that democracy; therefore, to overemphasize in the schools the tenets of a single religion is to disparage the meaning of democracy.

Each society is guilty of practicing the unenlightened arrogance of endorsing exclusively that which is familiar. The endorsement by a politician of the Ten Commandments, the Golden Rule, or the sayings of Confucius can be gauche or offensive, but always acceptable, in a democracy. If a politician advocates that one religion, or an aspect of one religion, should be emphasized in the school system to the exclusion of all others, the result would be the antithesis of education and certainly of democracy in action.

Steve Forbes's statement in that Des Moines high school, even though it is marginally acceptable, did not trigger my political support (I am convinced that this did not worry the candidate). Although Forbes has the right to advocate the importance of the Ten Commandments, I am concerned that his proposal might be implemented by the school system in Iowa. Display of the Ten Commandments in a public school would be subject to constitutional attack. If I thought that the Forbes candidacy would generate steam, I would have mobilized for action. In the meantime, I canceled my subscription to *Forbes* magazine.

THE SCHOOLS AND VOODOO

In 1995, students in the Bedford Central School District, which serves Westchester County in New York State, were introduced in the classroom to a strategy card game "Magic: The Gathering." Other school lessons followed: making models of Aztec gods; field trips to cemeteries; observing Earth Day; and making "worry dolls." In biology, the students analyzed the contents of an owl's stomach.

A few of the parents brought legal action against the school district (the "Satan Law Suit") alleging violation of freedom of religion through the references to voodoo, Satanism, and New Age spirituality. The parents also objected to drug and suicide counseling.

The American Catholic Lawyers Association joined the plaintiffs (parents) in attempting to eliminate these nefarious practices and references from the curriculum. Study of Darwin's *Origin of Species* violates the First Amendment of the Constitution, in the minds of some parents; however, the court did not support that reactionary contention. The lower district court supported the school district on fifteen of the eighteen counts. On appeal, the federal court, in 2002, reversed the trial court on the three remaining counts. Satan will continue to be discussed in the classroom.

Earth Day? Really! Imagine a dinner conversation with the agitated parents. Passionate fundamentalists are litigious while those balanced in thought control their emotions.

EDUCATION AND PUBLIC VOUCHERS

When public funds are used for private schools, the issue is clear. If the funds are devoted to parochial schools and used for religious purposes, the constitutional prohibition separating church and state applies. To hold to the contrary would provide a financial windfall for the Roman Catholic Church and would vitiate the will of the taxpayers.

If individual private vouchers are utilized, and the student selects the school, the issue has not been constitutional. Public policy issues arise. The public school system would be deprived of equivalent support, and the quality of the public schools would be further eroded.

Of equal importance, it is difficult for public officials to devise appropriate public policy standards for private, denominational schools. Schools featuring mythology in the curriculum would apply, and voucher-toting students could attend. The enforcement of minimal standards would be formidable.

On June 27, 2002, the U.S. Supreme Court, in a five-to-four decision, upheld the use of public funds for religious school tuition in the Cleveland, Ohio, voucher plan. The majority opinion of Chief Justice Rehnquist was the first important decision concerning religion since the Court held organized prayer in the schools to be unconstitutional forty years ago. This decision will not end the emotional debate regarding public vouchers for student tuition support. The debate will now be centered in the state courts. More than twenty-six states have rejected voucher proposals.

Under Cleveland's six-year-old program, 95 percent of the students using vouchers have enrolled in religious schools. Since the voucher program has a $2,250 cap on tuition, most of the students have enrolled in religious, rather than secular, schools, where the tuition is below the cap.

For example, Theodore Forstmann, a New York City financier renowned for his leveraged buyouts, has created a $170 million dollar fund to provide financial assistance for low-income families with children who wish to attend private schools. Forty thousand winners, selected by lottery from 1.2 million applicants, will receive $600 to $1,600 per year for four years. Matching donations of $1,000 will be required. Parochial school tuition approximates $2,500. Advertised as national in scope, New York City had 168,000 high school–level applicants (Chicago had 59,000 and Los Angeles had 54,000).

At the end of four years, the private plan does not integrate sustaining funds to enroll in higher educational institutions. In addition, there is no reference to class standing or the quality of the curriculum.

The Forstmann plan is the largest private effort in the country. The founder justifies his program as a challenge to the alleged monopoly of government in education.

In the United States diversity has been considered the hallmark at all levels of education. Additional competition is not the answer. Mr. Forstmann's plan, and comparable private plans, cannot be controlled legally. For the benefit of the public schools, donors should be requested to apply their grants to direct support for the public school system. Assisting students who may or may not be qualified, and who gain the privilege through lottery, is neither equitable nor wise.

EXTRACURRICULAR RELIGION

In 2000, the U.S. Court of Appeals in New York upheld the Milford Central School District's decision to disallow the Good News Club permission to offer prayer and Bible study as an extracurricular activity. The Good News Club is part of a national organization, the Child Evangelism Fellowship, which seeks to "evangelize boys and girls with the Gospel of the Lord Jesus Christ." The program is conducted after-school for six to twelve year old students who must obtain their parents' permission before participating.

The case was appealed to the U.S. Supreme Court, and in February 2001 the initial arguments were presented. The plaintiff alleged that it has a constitutional right to promote Bible study as an after-school activity on a comparable basis with other activities offered or endorsed by the public school system. The defendant maintains, as did the Court of Appeals, that the exclusion of the Good News Club was based on school policy not to endorse religious instruction and prayer as an extracurricular activity on school premises.

The initial reactions of the justices of the Supreme Court were divergent and confusing. Justice David Souter suggested that although precedent allows college students the right to sponsor religious services at public universities, comparable activities may not be acceptable for grade school children. Justice Antonin Scalia appeared to agree with the plaintiff and suggested that the activities of the Good News Club would not be "divisive in the community," and Justice Sandra Day O'Connor tended to concur.

On June 13, 2001, the U.S. Supreme Court, by a six-to-three vote, reversed the U.S. Court of Appeals. Justice Clarence Thomas wrote the majority opinion. The majority rejected the Court of Appeals decision that the First Amendment of the Constitution, guaranteeing the free exercise of religion and freedom of speech, supports the contention of the school district that the Good News Club religious activities would violate the constitutional rights of the other public school students.

This case represents another "hard case." Based on the reactions of several of the Supreme Court justices, "bad law" has emerged. In contemporary society in the United States, the rights of religious believers, and those who do not believe, are being constantly tested. Unfortunately, judicial interpretation will lack specificity when the Constitution and the Congress are silent. School administrators are continuing to make decisions in a public policy vacuum.

HIGHER EDUCATION AND CHURCH CONTROL

The character of the owners of a private higher educational institution is generally irrelevant in evaluating accreditation. The character of the owners is only germane if it impinges on the quality of the academic program. If the Vatican were to decree that all denominational colleges in the United States were precluded from teaching any religious credo other than Roman Catholicism, accreditation would not be in jeopardy until the curricula were altered to reflect the Vatican edict.

The Unification Church controls the University of Bridgeport in Connecticut. The Unification Church is an abbreviation for the Holy Spirit Association for the Unification of World Christianity, which was founded in 1954 in South Korea by the Reverend Sun Myung Moon.

If the leadership of the Unification Church at the University of Bridgeport assigned church personnel to the staff of the university who would be charged with converting students to membership in the church, without altering the curriculum, the accreditation would not be in jeopardy. If the church-assigned personnel altered the curriculum to limit freedom of expression, to impose thought control on the students, or to diminish the quality of the academic performance, accreditation would be in jeopardy.

During the 1960s, student and faculty agitation, in a few universities in the United States, threatened anarchy, deteriorating standards, or restricted freedoms. The threat of such actions did not affect accreditation. It is conceivable that the Unification Church recognizes the propaganda value of maintaining academic standards, including freedom of expression, in order to increase external donations and to secure additional converts.

At the University of Bridgeport, the fundamental error was to allow the financial plight of the university to obfuscate the judgment of the faculty and of the board of trustees. The accreditation process does not constitute a remedy. If academic standards are maintained at the University of Bridgeport, the "Moonies" will remain in control.

THE RHODE ISLAND "CHILDREN'S CRUSADE"

A decade ago, the Rhode Island Children's Crusade for Higher Education was founded to provide mentoring services, and a waiver of college tuition, for high school students who adhered to a reasonable code of conduct and academic attainment and who came from families with limited financial resources.

Since both of the historic "Children's Crusades" terminated in death or slavery for the participants, the choice of name in Rhode Island should have been subject to close scrutiny. Many citizens of the state were "turned off" because of the "crusade" terminology. On the other hand, a teenager with limited financial resources, in a state where the majority of the denizens are Roman Catholic, and after a parochial school education, cannot be expected to question the "crusader" designation.

Oh well, students at the College of the Holy Cross in Worcester, Massachusetts, are known as "Crusaders," and it does not appear to have affected their career perspective.

Moral standards are
created by men and
revised by history.

CREDO AND SENATOR LIEBERMAN

I n Detroit, during the 2000 presidential campaign, Democratic vice-presidential candidate Sen. Joseph Lieberman asserted that "we need to reaffirm our faith and renew the dedication of our nation and ourselves to God and God's purpose." According to press reports, he added: "We know that the Constitution wisely separates church from state, but remember: the Constitution guarantees freedom of religion not freedom from religion." Finally, he alleged that "without biblical traditions, the Ten Commandments, and the compassion, love, and inspiration of Jesus, it [the Constitution] could never have been written."

Senator Lieberman's position regarding the role of religion in the United States is troublesome. His allegations virtually duplicate those of the religious fundamentalists. He is parroting the credo of the religious right, which is predominantly Republican.

The media has ignored the fallacies in the senator's religious theme, which he would have applied to his role as vice president of the United States had he been elected to that office. Some Democrats welcomed the senator's position because it tended to counteract the moral turpitude represented by President Clinton.

The U.S. Constitution guarantees freedom of religion, which incorporates the freedom *not* to believe and to express points of view that may not comply with religious doctrine.

The First Amendment states that "Congress shall make no law respecting an establishment of religion, or prohibiting the free expression thereof." Article 6, paragraph 3 of the Constitution further provides that "no religious test shall ever be required."

In 1943, the U.S. Supreme Court, in *West Virginia State Board of Education* v. *Barnette*, held that the "freedom to differ is not limited to things that do not matter much. That would be a mere shadow of freedom. The test of its substance is the right to differ as to things that touch the heart of the existing order," including freedom *from* religion.

Several Supreme Court cases have held that the freedom of religion encompasses the freedom to express the antithesis of religion and to refrain from any form of religious observance or worship. Belief in God is not the constitutional basis of America: The basis is democracy, and the freedoms that derive from history, social mores, tradition, precedent, nurturing, reaction to arbitrary power, luck, common sense, and religious doctrine. The Ten Commandments did not dictate the version of democracy that was created in the United States.

Senator Lieberman can aver, with impunity, that there is need for an increased role for religion in public life, but when he dictates that the United States must renew its dedication "to God and God's purpose," he is ignoring the essence of freedom of religion and the separation of church and state.

"All men are created equal" is not yet a reality, and it certainly was not a reality at the time of Jesus or of the formulation of the Constitution. Freedom of speech and religion, and the quest for equality, may reflect religious traditions, but those traditions are not exclusive.

I cast my vote for Senator Lieberman because the principal option incorporated greater risk. At the same time, Senator Lieberman's religious dogma creates deep concern about his reading of history and his interpretation of the Constitution. If Vice President Gore had been elected president, and were he to die in office, the religious precepts of Senator Lieberman might present major issues regarding the separation of church and state.

In the remaining weeks of the campaign, given the lack of attention of the media and the electorate concerning substance, Senator Lieberman's statements regarding religion remained unaddressed.

GEORGE W. AND RELIGIOUS GRANTS

During the 2000 presidential campaign, discussions about the federal budget were occasionally described as "fuzzy." During the same campaign, George W. Bush endorsed a plan to make government grants to religious charities to support their local activities. In February 2001, as one of his first acts, President Bush created the Office of Faith-Based and Community Initiatives in the White House. Initial guidelines regarding potential grants to religious groups can also be characterized as "fuzzy."

President Bush has said that charities will not be forced to suppress their religious doctrine in order to secure government financing. Ostensibly, the objectives of his new program are to support the social work activities of religious groups and to increase private charitable giving.

After less than one month of operation, the White House Office of Faith-Based and Community Initiatives triggered opposition from the religious left and right.

Since presidential nominee Bush talked repeatedly about Jesus, most of the major religious groups assumed that the references to prayer endorsed Christian prayer and that the references to private school vouchers endorsed Christian schools. The Bush initiative to increase the role of religion in public life is now confronted with reality.

Government grants for religious charities have been supported for years by major conservative Christian leaders. Now that those grants may be implemented, doubts are beginning to emerge.

Rev. Pat Robertson, one of the most devoted advocates of the recommended program, has expressed serious reservations about the government financing religious movements that are outside the established order such as the Church of Scientology, the Wiccans, the Hare Krishna movement as well as the Unification Church, and a plethora of non-Western religions. Historically, government grants for major Catholic, Protestant, and Jewish organizations have been acceptable while minor groups, including non-Christian religions, have been denied access.

The Jewish Anti-Defamation League would like to deny grants to the Nation of Islam (Senator Lieberman has endorsed such grants), and the Reverend Louis Farrakhan has expressed the fear that if his Nation of Islam accepts a grant, it would obscure efforts of the administration to attract African Americans into the ranks of the Republican Party.

The director of the president's White House office muddied the waters by declaring that social service agencies that consider religious conversion the core of their program will not be eligible for government grants. Those programs might be assisted by individual grantees who receive government vouchers allowing them to select a beneficiary from a great array of religious organizations. It is probable that grants to groups to support a faith per se would be declared unconstitutional.

In 1996, the Charitable Choice legislation was passed as an integral component of the Welfare Reform Act. Charitable Choice mitigated several of the restrictions concerning government support for religious charities. In clarifying the grant-voucher dichotomy, and building on the Charitable Choice legislation, the White House office suggested that private, faith-based organizations engaged in housing rehabilitation would be eligible for federal grants, while organizations emphasizing religious conversion would only be eligible for voucher assistance from clients.

Within a few days of the White House pronouncement, the U.S. Agency for International Development informed an evangelical recipient of a grant for constructing emergency housing in El Salvador that it "must maintain adequate and sufficient separation between prayer sessions and its USAID-funded activities" (housing). This distinction was communicated to the grantee after work had begun in El Salvador.

The USAID pronouncement and the White House distinction between grants and vouchers have provoked further concerns from religious spokespersons. The groups are worried that if they accept a grant, there may be a tendency for the government to control the programs it subsidizes. Government impingement on alleged religious integrity and government support of religious movements that transcend the Judeo-Christian tradition, constitute the gravamen of the growing opposition.

It would appear that the initial sense of well-being of having a president of the United States who champions the role of religion and religious groups in American society may be subject to revision. Now that the administration is beginning to focus on the separation of church and state, and the complexity of religious expression, it may be difficult for the White House to distinguish religious friends from enemies.

FREE INSTITUTIONS IN A FREE SOCIETY

In a free society the people express disdain for many of their institutions. The health of our free institutions, and the integrity of the leaders who represent those institutions, must be encouraged and protected (as long as they warrant positive treatment). Excluding the police power, which is relevant in emergency situations, free institutions constitute the ultimate strength of a free society.

For example, the media guarantee a modicum of free speech. Individual citizens, to maintain their perceived status, seldom express free speech in public. Unless you are a performer, a quack, or a member of a fringe group, the risk to one's reputation is inordinate. For an individual, the penalty is ostracism rather than incarceration or banishment. It is possible for individuals to exercise free speech publicly, but only once (and you should count very carefully).

In contrast, free institutions, exercising basic rights, have relative autonomy and more effective tools at their disposal. Rather than disparaging free institutions, private citizens should attend meetings, serve on committees, vote informatively, and present a vanguard against irrational external attacks on the free institutions (e.g., colleges, churches, the media, etc.) that distinguish a democracy from a totalitarian state.

GOD AND COMMUNISM

The affirmation of the existence of God, and the revelation of the truth of scripture, are concepts not dissimilar from the psychological motivation that induced Communists to corroborate the infallibility of Stalin and the goal of Communist world domination. They are also comparable to persecuted cold-war Communists confessing to deviations and crimes that were mere fiction.

Religious beliefs are based on the tenet that righteousness flows from the comprehension of the incomprehensible. A belief in God, or an equivalent Communist or other secular deity, is illogical and confounds human progress. The propensity to confirm precise belief in the unknown negates the necessity for original thought and perpetuates tyranny in society, government, and religion.

PSEUDORELIGION

Every five years,
a human being acquires
a new set of atoms,
not attitudes.

THE GOSPEL OF SENTIENCE

If I were psychotic enough to create a new religion (many friends are convinced that I qualify), I would take a few pages from the book of Buddhism and decree that all living things are created equal. Plants and trees would be considered sentient, and elderly ladies who talk to the African violets in their kitchens would be initiated into the priesthood (alienating a goodly number of organized religious sects).

I realize that the ultimate ritual of my newly launched sect would be emulation of the oriental priests who refuse to walk on grass or garden paths for fear of terminating the life cycle of an ant. Little do the priests realize that walking on concrete may insure the demise of thousands of living organisms considerably smaller than ants.

Even with total acceptance of my religious credo, a gnat may be inadvertently destroyed or automobile headlights may annihilate a few moths, but the underlying religious precept would be clear and inviolate. With each cut of a chainsaw, there is an unheard cry of pain.

I am being absurd, like all religious prophets, but in fact, my religious credo is only marginally inane. If we respected every form of life enough to care about the quality of death for all living things, and if we cared about the feelings of living things for which we have yet to authenticate sensibility, each person might manifest more sympathy for others of the species.

To carry sentience to a ludicrous extreme, if you do not endorse my concept of sentience, you will not be eligible for Heaven.

ZEN AND NATURE

Because of the absence of a deity, religious dogma, or the fiction associated with Christ, Mohammed, or Buddha, Zen has superficial appeal. It represents a simple, uncomplicated philosophy, and the back-to-nature approach creates more than minimal attraction.

Zen is anti-intellectual, therefore, it generally fails to meet the essential needs of the only rational animal. If all of our progenitors had practiced Zen, fire would never have been discovered, abortion would still represent accident, and we would not have been rewarded with an outstanding slate of candidates for national office.

Without intellectual challenge, a philosophy of life may be doomed to extinction or at least irrelevance. That is the major reason Christianity has survived. It may be irrational to believe the basic tenets of the Christian faith, but it requires a certain amount of acumen to embrace, reject, or ignore the message.

Of equal importance, Zen's preoccupation with the natural is artless and unadorned. Such a belief could only emerge from anti-intellectualism, which takes us back to Zen.

Nature is complicated, competitive, unfair, and violent. Zen devotees believe just the opposite. Invariably, they take refuge in the simplicity of nature, which in fact is the antithesis of that notion. Zen paintings depict an unreal natural state where there is no conflict, strain, or change. Scientific discovery has extended the complexity of nature and illustrated our limited, but increasing, understanding of the universe.

Finally, Zen fails to recognize a fundamental truth. Without an ethical base, which distinguishes right from wrong, even if the standards are erroneous, human beings will be unable to survive in association with each other. Social interaction, including the family, the clan, the class, and the race, to say nothing of the city or the nation-state, are dependent upon a learned differentiation between right and wrong.

When the mother spanks the child, even if she is "wrong," as long as she is consistent in applying punitive measures, discipline is being dispensed based on a perceived, or soon to be perceived, ethical system. To advocate that anything goes, which is the philosophical position of Zen, ignores reality. Social rules, based on some form of ethics, have insured man's survival (at least until the nuclear age).

YOGA

After listening to a friend extol the virtues of slow-motion, nonviolent exercise, I finally began the "twenty-eight-day plan." Yoga is not really a big deal. It has only altered the course of my life.

After the first day, my arthritis disappeared, my gout was gone, the tendonitis in my shoulder had vanished, my sebaceous cysts subsided, seven pounds were missing, and the scars from my operations appeared virile rather than venal. Naturally, I can hardly wait for the second lesson.

Seriously, the Yoga approach to exercise makes intrinsic good sense. Total concentration on the physical movement; stretching without pain; slow, deliberate movements to minimize the potential of injury; and holding extended positions to induce increased mobility are eminently sound prescriptions.

The meditative corollary may be less convincing. Unifying self with the ultimate principle sounds a bit like the preaching that other religious factions employ with different words of art.

RELIGION OR AN OPIATE

Religion does not represent an opiate, per Lenin, but only an irrelevancy that creates meaningless but explosive schisms. In the absence of definitive proof, which may never materialize, religious zealots will continue to agitate, provoking the inevitable Belfasts. Religious adherents will continue to follow religious advocates (even when those advocates fail to honor religious and moral codes).

The rest of us who would prefer something more palatable, or even nothing, to worship will continue to remain silent. This represents the usual demeanor when religious zealots enjoy basic freedoms.

A TOUCH OF ASTROLOGY

Speaking of rationality, there is very little associated with astrology. In Suzanne White's *The New Astrology* (New York: St. Martin's, 1986), the author merges the Western reliance upon the heavens for the interpretation of the person with the oriental reliance upon variables on Earth (such as dogs and dragons). Using Ms. White's amalgamated charts, I have determined that I am a heavenly Aquarius and an earthly dragon.

Now for the difficult part. There are 144 different Heaven and Earth variables; therefore, differences among human beings are confined to that number. As you might expect, the words of art used to describe each of the categories could apply equally to every human being. The lack of precision in the use of terms is frightening. The credulity of the believers is staggering.

Human beings will endorse any dogma that preaches hope and reassurance in a partially structured format. I am a dog for saying it. You are a rat for disagreeing. So much for the scripture!

SUPERSTITION

The upper atmospheric winds have generated the insidious symptoms of Bavarian foehn. During foehn, because of the strong negative vibes, Munich surgeons will not perform operations. Walking to the office, on a foehn day, and following a premonition, I crossed a street earlier than was my wont in order to insure that an expectation would materialize. As a teenager, I was convinced that if I did not place my foot on a crack in a stretch of sidewalk, I would return the opening kickoff at the next football game for one hundred and four yards.

In maturity, there are still occasional "lucky" charms. Wearing a particular shirt, completing a chore in a prescribed way, or tacking on a mile to the normal evening run, might insure access to a minor prize. Oh yes, if I make it through the traffic light, before it changes to red, it may lead to a positive result in another sphere. The figurative "cracks" in life are acts of obeisance to the supernatural. At the risk of being misunderstood, a belief in God might generate a close analogy.

Nearly all of us invoke a form of beneficence to improve the odds, in a cultural or personal context, to insure that sickness, accident, "bad luck," or other potential negative happenings will not occur or that corresponding positive developments will be assured.

Superstition reflects an irrational belief that may have significance in a moment of need. Quite often, we hope to provide a boost for anticipated good fortune. I am still tempted by the serendipity of superstition. If you would acknowledge that your religious beliefs relate to the same mystical base as my superstition, I would be encouraged. Beware of the "evil eye"!

RANDOMNESS

When you consider the randomness of life, do not confine your thoughts to the luck of the die. The manifestations of randomness, good or bad, depending upon your perspective, are infinite—one of millions of spermatozoa that produced you; one of the few survivors in a tragic airplane crash; one of the millions living in Somalia, Kosovo, Indonesia, or Grosse Point, Michigan; one of the porpoises that avoided the tuna net.

The randomness that dictates our personal lifestyle is also important. On which side of your face will skin cancer appear? Will your current diet or pill intake prove counterproductive? Will running prolong your life? Will reading restrict your sight? Which fork in the road, or at the table, should you take?

In life, the only thing more important than randomness is genes. The only thing more important than genes is environment. The only thing more important than environment is your choice of parents. The only thing more important than parents is good fortune. Good fortune is based on religious principles, superstition, luck, or to repeat myself, randomness.

EUTHANASIA

Our Labrador retriever is dead. After fifteen years of unmitigated faithfulness, always giving more joy than he received, he succumbed with characteristic dignity to the ravages of age. Tad (somehow, the name suited him) had deteriorated appreciably, and his infirmities were acute: heartworm, a persistent cough, loss of hearing and eyesight, arthritis, and the serious atrophy of the hip bones (a Lab curse), which made walking and getting up and down a painful experience.

For the last six months of his life, we assumed that Tad would be able to "hang on," and he did. We deluded ourselves into believing that his pain was controlled, and that the periods of partial mobility were more than acts of courage. A few weeks before his death, he was partially incontinent, a major concern for a proud animal. It was necessary to lift him in and out of the automobile. We carried him with the use of a sling, and yet, until the end, he managed to crawl up and down the stairs to spend the night near us. Without fail, he rose to the challenge of food. On the morning of his death, he ate a hearty breakfast. The debilities of the body never affected his equable disposition or his kindness to the outside world.

On the night prior to his death, Tad was barely able to move. For the first time I realized that we were prolonging Tad's life to fulfill our own needs. The pain was significant. After a sleepless night, I realized that euthanasia was the gentle answer to Tad's needs.

The shot was administered by the veterinarian. That simple sentence summarizes a very emotional experience. The absence of my spouse exacerbated the grief. Euthanasia, in theory, is a pragmatic option for all sensate things; however, making the decision to put that theory into practice was agonizing. For an animal that had become a member of the family, but one for which the communication factors were limited, the difficulties were compounded.

For months, I had seen Tad in every endearing pose, from every vantage point. He was raised with the children, and he matured as they did. His distinctive characteristics were embedded in the physical surroundings we all enjoyed.

Tad was a prince in both the regal and comparative sense. He demanded very little except our full commitment. In return, he provided continuity, affection, and joy in a world where those attributes are in short supply.

For Tad, a dog's life was based on acceptance and caring. For those of us left behind, Tad will be remembered as a unique friend, a satisfying companion, and a loving presence that lived life to the fullest. Tad represented daily proof that man's best friend is his dog.

Based on the Tad precedent, should euthanasia be applied to a human being?

AN ANIMAL BILL OF RIGHTS

In Sweden, a bill of rights has been considered for animals. In the United States, the reaction, if there is a reaction, will be negative — "those socialists are idiotic" — but take a moment for reflection.

If birds and animals (and even trees) do not qualify for Heaven, should the concept of everlasting life be as attractive? When you recognize the extent to which farm animals, and even domestic pets, are abused, is it not logical to invoke the protection of God, for the long haul, and of the judicial system here on Earth?

I realize that an Animal Bill of Rights might be subject to abuse and misinterpretation. It would impose restrictions, some of which might be onerous, in order to insure humane treatment. Bashing cows on the head with a sledge hammer has been discontinued at the Chicago stock yards. If we have been able to provide more humane methods to sacrifice animals for meat eaters, we have taken one small step for animalkind.

If my dog cannot have access to Heaven, I am not certain that I want to qualify for the privilege. On the other hand, if animals will need lawyers to interpret their earthly rights, the Animal Bill of Rights will be in jeopardy.

FUNERALS

14

Funerals should honor the living not the dead. *

A FUNERAL ORATION

At age seventy-two, a neighbor died of cancer. His life was full. His assignments were meaningful. His travels were constant. His impact on his surroundings was positive.

During the funeral service at a local church, the man of the cloth revealed that the spouse of the deceased had confided in a telephone conversation that she believed in the resurrection. Revealing that confidence was unethical. Assuming that the spouse's view of the hereafter was relevant to the proceedings, imposing personalized religious credo on a grieving, interdenominational gathering was gross and inappropriate.

Subsequently, at a postservice dinner, I asked a man of the cloth who was present at the funeral service for his professional reaction. He agreed that the preacher in question was practicing his trade in an unethical manner.

At the service, the son of the deceased read a few lines from an obscure author the content of which I am certain the deceased would not have appreciated or endorsed. The gist of the reading suggested that the people on Earth are divided into two camps—rich and poor. I suppose that the simplistic dichotomy should have been ignored; however, the rich were equated with power and rectitude and the poor with impotence and plodding irrelevance. The son of the deceased then pontificated that his father would have fit nicely into the second category. I believe that I heard a giggle from the casket.

I trust the judgment of my survivors, but if they speak about the departed subsequent to my demise, I would be reassured if they would avoid a church pulpit as the situs of their remarks. More meaningfully, I would be grateful if they would make a special effort to position me with the rich and powerful (even though that assertion stretches the truth appreciably). Since I hope to be cremated, I can only express the wish that the circular doors will encircle the remains in privacy.

A THANKSGIVING BLESSING

On Thanksgiving Day, the minister at a local chapel delivered his final sermon before retirement. Because of limited heat in the room, he wore a dirty, crumpled raincoat. That observation is interesting but irrelevant. The sermon was a disaster.

The minister read the first few chapters of Genesis through God's respite on the seventh day. Without transition, he then read from a James Michener tome that illustrated the diversity of Earth's habitats. Without transition, he cited Carl Sagan's works dealing with the complexity of the universe and the fleeting moment that represents recorded history. Without transition, he expressed gratitude to God for things large, small, bright, and beautiful (without attribution to a Scottish veterinarian). Without transition, he quoted a few lines from Emerson thanking God for specific beautiful things, and without transition, he asked the congregation whether anyone had lost an umbrella. Finally, without transition, he called for the offering.

Another golden opportunity was lost by a spokesperson for the organized church. Most of the congregation seemed superficially pleased with the sermon.

PERICLES' FUNERAL ORATION

When I was taking a college course in public speaking, I read Pericles' Funeral Oration as reported by Thucydides. I treasured one quotation: "For it is only human for men not to bear praise of others beyond the point at which they can hope to rival their exploits."

Years later, I felt that the Pericles quotation might have been in error. I obtained the pertinent source and read: "For men can endure to hear others praised only so long as they persuade themselves of their own ability to equal the actions recounted: when this point is passed, envy comes in and with it incredulity." A superior translation confirms the tenor of Thucydides recording of Pericles.

Based on my exposure to *Homo sapiens*, I would now venture to suggest that grounds for praise among Greeks in the fifth century B.C. were related to a different perception of the other guy's ability or attainment. In fact, we contemporaries are willing to praise the other person for virtually any feat that we cannot emulate. When my territory of alleged competence is transgressed, envy becomes a useful trait.

For example, I swallow hard when I hear another person reflecting my professional fields of endeavor being praised for excellence in those fields. On the other hand, I am willing to endorse Tiger Woods's golfing sovereignty with alacrity.

It is not surprising that Pericles received little immediate acclaim for his address on behalf of the fallen Athenian military heroes. The privates were envious of the generals rather than the corporals, and they lost their perspective. In spite of translation difficulties, modern funeral sermons seldom capture a thought worth remembering.

A CREMATION SERVICE

At a Bavarian cremation, I was appalled by the German farewell to the departed. At the conclusion of the nonsectarian ritual, huge circular steel doors slowly enveloped the remains of the deceased. The outer immobile walls were ten feet high and one foot thick. As the circular doors closed tightly on the deceased, the mourners assumed from the ambience that his or her friend or loved one had been relegated to the alternate place other than Heaven.

If our deceased friend had attended the service, on our side of the walls, he would have laughed. The cremation was nonsectarian, but the religious significance was manifest.

A FAREWELL TO THE DECEASED

At a church in central New York State, I attended a particularly taste-less funeral ceremony. The deceased was a very special friend who made significant contributions and was treasured by many. The service was arranged by the family, and if the deceased had attended, I am certain that he would have been appalled.

As usual, the preacher was painfully culture-bound and lacking in imagination or feeling. He reminded me of the chaplain of the U.S. Senate who recently prayed that God would ordain "sound delibera-tions" in the Senate chamber. The central New York version of official church representation admonished us "to give thanks for the life of the deceased." The minister did not know the deceased. More important, he made no effort to discover why that life could be distinguished from the six billion others who might have been in the same terminal position and for whom we might extend gratitude.

As a pallbearer, I was one of eight men (equality of gender has not yet invaded funerals) who was selected to transport the remains for fifty feet from the altar to the deluxe vehicle owned by the funeral director. I felt that I was participating in a shopping center rite devoid of feeling or significance.

THE IRISH WAKE

Funerals should honor the living not the dead. The Irish wake captures the appropriate sentiment. Since the survivors are cognizant of their own good fortune in continuing the game of life, they are not predis-posed to lose the opportunity to sing their own praises as they mouth the words of the designated psalm.

The survivors determine the format and the content of the ritualistic components, which are orchestrated to honor the deceased. In fact, the immediate family is using the death of a loved one to provide the therapy, after a significant loss, to expedite the continuation of living.

Funerals should provide a structure for frivolous social interaction. The emphasis should be placed on the living, the imponderables of life, and the pure pleasure that must fill the void that meaning has failed to occupy. Laughter and an occasional tear, provoked by that laughter rather than the passing of a loved one, should constitute the order of a funeral day.

THE RITUALS OF DEATH

Mother Teresa is dead. Universal reaction to her death appears to be nonsectarian and heartfelt.

Mother Teresa was born in Macedonia. After a brief stint as a nun in Ireland, in 1946, she went to Calcutta, India. For one-half century, she ministered to the needs of the impoverished in India, where she founded the Missionaries of Charity, whose membership grew significantly. In 1979, Mother Teresa was awarded the Nobel Peace Prize. Her work has received positive reactions from the media and from the laity in the developed and in the lesser-developed world. Although the religious overtones were excessive, her death, and the significance of her life, were treated in a rational manner.

One week after the death announcement, the pope decreed that procedural rules would be ignored, and that Mother Teresa would probably be formally endorsed for immediate sainthood.

As I understand it, beatification certifies, following the requisite investigation, that the deceased is in Heaven. Canonization proceeds a step further. The deceased is not only officially in Heaven, but he or she is also certified, as a saint, to intercede in Heaven on behalf of sinners. In any event, the Catholic Church has responded with alacrity to universal popularity rather than to the documented saintly works of the deceased.

Mother Teresa led a quiet, constructive, exemplary life. She acted like a saint, but I regret that the Catholic Church will rush to sanctify that designation.

"HAVE A GOOD (FUNERAL) DAY"

An advertisement in a local newspaper included a photograph of nineteen overweight, smiling people with an affirmative action component of Hispanics. "From our family to yours" was the lead followed by "Wishing you a safe and enjoyable Fourth of July weekend. Please don't drink and drive." The sponsoring organization was named and designated, a "professional service for people who care." The Web site was thoughtfully provided. It was a bit disturbing when "Family Funeral Service" was subsequently displayed in the ad.

Death is a reality with which all families must deal. To combine a burial service with the values associated with a picnic is the epitome of bad taste. The company should be selling caskets coupled with a modicum of solace.

Since I have chosen cremation, I do not have a personal stake; however, I resent the "have a nice day" advertising pitch related to a very personal, important family rite. I identify with the wake as a celebration of life, but I deeply resent a photograph emulating a twenty-year high school reunion being utilized as a "come-on" for routine funeral services. I wonder if the company gives green stamps.

FUNERALS AND ORGANS

At a funeral service for Donald Gramm, the Metropolitan Opera baritone, which was held at Avery Fisher Hall at Lincoln Center, on June 20, 1983, the organ prelude was superb. Previously, I had seldom heard the organ played by a consummate musician. At a variety of churches and theaters, I have lived through the feeble efforts of organists who never came to terms with their instrument. The repetitive church hymns, played by less than accomplished organists, created a prejudice against that instrument (only the nonclassical guitar has produced a comparable negative reaction).

At the service, Charles Bressler sang the lovely "Dist du bei mir" by Bach; Richard Stilwell sang "Stopping by the Woods on a Snowy Evening," and Judith Raskin sang "An die Musik" by Schubert. Sarah Caldwell illustrated vividly, and with a deft light touch, the warmth and humor of the departed. Beverly Sills spoke with deep feeling about his humanity and humility.

If there must be a funeral service, the agenda should honor the sensibilities of the congregation, as well as the deceased. Appropriately selected music, accomplished musicians, superb speakers, and a few light moments should be featured.

FAITH AND DEATH

Religious faith feeds on observance of death. The scriptures are replete with references to death. The fact that many cemeteries adjoin churches represents more than historic accident.

If death were not a dominant factor in dogma, most religious credos would dissolve through inertia. Because we cannot yet prove that death is final, the deception continues.

APPROACHING DEATH GRACEFULLY

When the end comes, I hope that it will not be badly acted. The longer I survive the more I realize that form should not take a back seat to substance. Whether we are contemplating the apocalypse or a lesser production, the exit should be handled with aplomb and a smattering of "show biz." When we are born, we have no control over the dramatic quality of the performance. In contemplation of death, if the mental condition allows, experience and humility should dictate a meaningful withdrawal.

It seems that the secret of a graceful adjustment to old age is to ignore the inevitability, and the pain, of physical and mental deterioration. That prescription leaves little hope for a major breakthrough in coping with the debilitating process of longevity. Your friends will die or fade away. The next generation will shun the advice that flows from experience. As life ebbs, take the requisite time to prepare for an exit that is gracious, stylish, and understated. Finally, remember your lines.

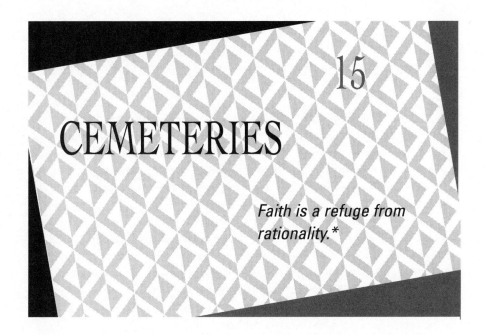

CEMETERIES

15

Faith is a refuge from rationality. *

A PLACE FOR PERMANENT REST**

Although I do not adhere to any specific religious credo, and although I consider God, and all other past and present gods, figments of humankind's vivid imagination, a stroll in a cemetery can evoke unique thoughts and sensations that transcend respect for the dead or interest in familial snatches of history. A cemetery is a situs where it is easy to be reflective and difficult to be cynical. For decades, I have enjoyed visiting quaint little rural cemeteries because they provide a private, fresh air exposure to history, and there is not any requirement to identify with the remnants below.

I am not impressed by the putative spirits of the dead, the symbolism of human burial rights, or the asserted presence of poltergeists. I am impressed by the transience of life, the "quiet despair" of most individual lives, and the nuggets of historic fact that come "alive" in the ambience of the collected dead.

In a cemetery, I have an uncontrolled urge to take notes; a burning desire to write creatively, and a conviction that some humans, because of

131

their unique and/or positive exploits, should be excused from cremation. I have no interest in having my burial plot visited, but I have been stimulated by the plots and inscriptions that some of our ancestors have utilized.

The family dimension regarding cemeteries is also intriguing. In a rural Virginia cemetery, my father and mother, both sets of grandparents, and three aunts and an uncle are buried in adjoining plots. The cemetery is very basic and very rural, and when close family members are involved, nostalgia and a sense of caring are intertwined with the history lesson.

At the World War I American cemetery at Aise-Oisne in France, for the first time since visiting the graves of my family, and the Unknown Soldier's Tomb at Arlington, Virginia, my reaction was emotional. Because all of the markers were identical, and because they appeared to be infinite in number, the vulnerability and idiocy of humankind seemed palpable. There is nothing more touching than being near dead soldiers resting where they fell.

I believe that cremation is the only solution for humankind. It is most reassuring to be able to pay homage to the ones you love, or to amorphous history, at a precise spot in the open air, rather than to a jar which merely notes their prior existence. I shall miss the subjective pangs and historic stimulation of a periodic cemetery visit, but I believe that the time has come to convert all cemeteries into glorious parks. Until I secure the votes for that transformation, I will continue to pay my respects to those who preceded us, at unpretentious rural cemeteries.

MILITARY GRAVES IN FRANCE

In France, in the area of Varennes on the Aisne River, the road passes a score of inadequately designated, and virtually ignored, French, British, German, and American World War I military cemeteries. The number of simple graves is depressing, and the folly of war is poignant. The religious significance of the plots is unexpressed, except for a few citations on several of the more costly tombstones.

At Varennes, there are several unattractive stone monuments placed in memory of a Pennsylvania military unit that suffered extensive casualties. Since few tourists traverse this route, spring flowers draped over the simple graves would have been fitting. In contrast, the

German cemeteries in the region are attractive, reflect a reassuring scale, and accentuate flowers rather than granite.

The manicured American World War I cemetery near Chateau-Thierry, and the unattended, seldom-visited German cemetery in close proximity, without evoking religious credo, represent a comprehensible scale of ultimate human sacrifice. Belleau Wood is still filled with shrapnel, and the metal continues to attract lightning in a storm. When a metal fragment works its way to the surface, four score and six years after the battle, lockjaw is a threat to the handler.

A military cemetery warrants respect. It is unnecessary to add the trappings of religious credo to the burden of those who died in defense of national honor, right or wrong.

World Leaders at Bitburg

In July 1985, President Ronald Reagan visited the Bitburg Cemetery in West Germany. Hundreds of German soldiers who lost their lives in World War II are buried at Bitburg. In addition, a few SS troopers are interred at the same location.

President Reagan's intelligence contingent was unable to obtain translations of the tombstones of the SS members; therefore, the Reagan advance party was unaware that their presence sullied the ambience.

At the invitation of West German chancellor Helmut Kohl, President Reagan and the chancellor completed a short walk in Bitburg Cemetery. Demonstrators were omnipresent, and the press accentuated the terrible impact of the Holocaust.

Without being required to perform a litmus test on every grave occupant, world leaders should be encouraged to visit military cemeteries. Graves are filled to commemorate the dead. When markers are placed on those graves, they signify that somebody cares.

Out of respect to the host country, a guest leader should not refuse to visit a military cemetery. It is an act of human decency to pay homage to a former enemy, who has become a friend, and who has lost a significant component of the next male generation in a global conflict. Politics must end with burial. Discomforting reminders of war may serve as a partial deterrent to future wars.

CEMETERIES AND PROGENITORS

Sixteen miles East of Orange, in northern Virginia, the Antioch Baptist Church, a white, clapboard building, is nestled near the adjoining forest. The church was organized in 1833. The present building was erected in 1909. The setting is rural, and there is no indication that the last two centuries have affected the appearance of the church or the content of its doctrine.

Beside the church, in the center of a small cemetery lot, there is a monument, with a crown-top, where my maternal great-grandparents are buried. The side of the monument bears the following inscription: "Blessed are the dead which die in the Lord." A few feet from the monument, there is a smaller marker that serves as the grave of my mother's maternal uncle and aunt.

For many generations, this rural church has been a reassuring home for its congregation, from baptism to burial. If the Antioch Church and its cemetery did not exist, I would have been exposed to less of my heritage.

I am grateful that the Antioch Church has allowed me to establish meaningful roots; however, the inscription on the larger monument provides little solace for many of us who remain.

CREMATION

Many years ago, my mother-in-law was cremated. For two years, her ashes remained in an urn at my father-in-law's residence. My wife's mother had expressed the wish, in addition to cremation, that her ashes be spread at a desert park. As her husband's medical condition deteriorated, we decided not to delay the final request.

The desert park was created to protect the natural environment surrounding two peaks that offer a major view of Phoenix. The zoo is located in the park, and my wife's mother enjoyed the animals and the view.

The cremated ashes were scattered under a lonely tree on the western side of the southern peak. Smog and industrial development have curtailed the view; however, the desert still predominates, and the site is infinitely superior to an unattractive cemetery cluttering the urban landscape.

As we stood enjoying the desert air, and listening to the cactus wrens and United Airlines jets, it was a pleasure to invoke the memory of a family member and to take solace in the fact that her wish had been honored.

In retrospect, scattering ashes in a desert park, without a permit, probably constitutes a misdemeanor. The greater violation is to extend the private land devoted to cemetery use. Such designation represents an inane use of limited urban space, esthetic blight, and the omnipresence of ugly stones that merely differentiate the deceased by the affluence of the surviving family members.

HAPPY HUNTING GROUNDS **

A delightful walk through the historic town of Stockbridge, Massachusetts, was relaxing and edifying. In the eighteenth century, our progenitors were much less covetous of realty than we. All buildings on the main street were set back at least thirty yards from the road. Subsequent generations discarded this wise policy and constructed impermanent (a cultural trait) buildings within a few feet of the municipal main streets. Stockbridge and Litchfield, Connecticut, are two surviving examples of sagacious colonial planning.

After enjoying the town hall, and visiting the old church, which at 11:00 A.M. on a weekday was open to the world, we wandered by the oldest cemetery in town. In one section, the historic markers were identified as "Indian Christians."

Is it not ludicrous that three hundred and fifty years after our unethical forefathers seized western Massachusetts from the initially peaceful Indians, we commemorate the few impressionable native sons and daughters who were converted to Christianity? Would it not have been more fitting to venerate the noble chiefs who ruled wisely, as animists, for generations; and the brave warriors who carried a significant number of paleface scalps with them to the Happy Hunting Grounds?

It would be a novel and reassuring experience to visit an Indian burial ground where a totem pole or other marker read: "Here lies a White pagan who believed in our Gods."

CHURCH ESTHETICS

When you feel discouraged, think of the men and women "of the cloth." *

THE PLACE FOR RELIGION**

Without place references religious orders might not survive. Only the Muslims are able to engage in group prayer without a holy roof, and even they face toward Mecca. When Brigham Young, following the instructions of the Angel Moroni, trekked to that great desert in the West, he exclaimed: "This is the place."

The "Wailing Wall" provides solace for the Jews. The Druids of southern England drew radial lines pointing someplace, and the Crusaders were heading for the "Holy Land." In the absence of meaningful substance (theses that are subject to proof), religious orders are forced to invent places that become surrogates for substance.

When we "go to church," we are honoring a place. Superstition can only thrive when there are tangible trappings of trivia. Whatever the icon (e.g., a cross, beads, or a Buddhist wheel), we are merely taking part of "the place" with us.

When, or if, a religious precept can be pegged to reality, or subject to proof, that reality will sustain us without resorting to place identification.

CATHEDRALS AND BEAUTY

Without an extensive history, beautiful structural manifestations of religion in the United States are limited. The Mormons represent the only significant new sect in North America. The Mormon temples in Salt Lake City and on Oahu are impressive, but compared to a religious edifice in Europe, the historic relevance is marginal. Without the structures of religion, European history would be less meaningful, but cathedrals express a paucity of intellectual and architectural freedom for the converted masses.

With significant exceptions, the only urban structure throughout Europe that warrants a Michelin reference, or has earned a directional road marker, is the cathedral. Whether the cathedral is Romanesque or Gothic, thirteenth century or sixteenth century, built on a hill or on an island, the themes are repetitive and unimaginative.

If God is omnipotent, he or she would want earthly manifestations of devotion to him or her to be expressed in infinite variety. Even within the relatively narrow scope of Christianity, one would anticipate that the wayward architectural believer might conjure up a user-friendly little structure with a soft seat for meditation; a large picture window in the nave to commemorate God's work on Earth; and an open, glassed ceiling to anticipate God's conditional invitation to Heaven.

Let us leave the belfries to the bats, the abbeys to the professionals, and the cathedrals to those who have repudiated a continuing intellectual search. God must prefer his or her chosen ones to worship him or her in the ambience of hope and beauty rather than in a profusion of stained glass.

Diversity in art, and the existing cathedrals, are antitheses.

FRANCE

Paris

Sacre-Coeur

The basilica of the Sacre-Coeur at Montmarte in Paris was begun in 1876, completed in 1910, and consecrated in 1919. The Romano-Byzantine style, by Adadie and other architects, is modern, yet, the clean lines and unprecedented setting afford an extraordinary sight.

In 1944, the stained glass was destroyed by German bombing, but the beautiful, white equestrian statues of Saint Louis and Joan of Arc have survived. The thirty-mile panoramic view of Paris from the front steps of the basilica is unexcelled.

St. Eustache

Adjoining Les Halles in Paris, the singular St. Eustache Church represents Gothic architecture and Renaissance decoration. Begun in 1214, the structure is dedicated to a Roman general who saw a cross between a stag's antlers, was converted by the experience, and was sanctified for his exemplary vision. Because of its central location, St. Eustache became the choice for public rites including the funerals of Moliere and Comte de Mirabeau. The church also reflects a long-term commitment to choral and organ music including the first performances of nineteenth-century pieces composed by Franz Liszt and Louis-Hector Berlioz.

St. Denis

On a cold day in January, I visited the Basilique St. Denis located north of the city center of Paris. The streets were slippery, and the inside of the Cathedral was bitter cold.

In the seventh century, the cathedral was constructed as an abbey over the tomb of St. Denis. It is alleged that St. Denis carried his decapitated head for a considerable distance. For that feat, he was rewarded with the distinction as the patron saint of France.

In the twelfth century, the church was rebuilt as the first church in the Gothic style. Subsequently, that style was emulated at Chartres. The stained glass windows are renowned. Unfortunately, on a cloudy day, the external light was inadequate for a full display.

The huge crypt is the situs for the tombs of all of the French kings for twelve centuries (from 629 to 1824). The immediate families of several kings are also included. Having just finished Hilaire Belloc's biography of Marie Antoinette, I was particularly intrigued that she is also entombed at St. Denis.

The history incorporated in the crypt of the Basilique St. Denis illustrates the unparalleled power and influence of the Roman Catholic Church.

Chartres

Approaching Chartres, with the summer's first rays of glorious sunshine illuminating the cathedral from a distance of twenty kilometers, the asymmetrical spires, from different architectural periods, conveyed a mystical, dare I say, "religious" quality. Since reading Henry Adams's pseudo-architectural treatise, which was prepared for the impending visit of his nieces, I had wanted to pay my respects to the majestic structure at Chartres.

The "Cult of the Virgin" dominates the history of the shrine, one of the oldest in Europe. One belfry was constructed in the twelfth century, and the Romanesque steeple has remained intact for eight hundred years. The other steeple is Gothic, and the combination is overpowering and basically unappealing. The interiors of most French cathedrals are cluttered, damp, and uninviting. If the benefits of piety were correlated with comfort, and an attractive interior, French cathedrals would not have survived.

Le Mont-Saint-Michel

On the coast, between Brittany and Normandy, is Mont-Saint-Michel, one of the most stirring sights in Europe. Virtually circular, the 3,000 foot granite island is surrounded by sand (some of which is quick). Only at high tide does the mountain become an island. A one-hundred-yard causeway connects the island to the mainland. In the early nineteenth century, Napoleon converted the site to a prison, which it remained for half a century.

A winding narrow street, primarily for pedestrians, rises to the abbey above. The street is lined with small hotels and many unattractive tourist shops, a large number of which were constructed in the fifteenth century. The approach to the abbey is filthy, and the Coney Island–like hawkers, and rude tourists, do not provide the most auspicious introduction. For the devout, the entrance to the abbey must test the depth of faith.

Construction of the abbey was begun in the eighth century. Some sections were not completed until the nineteenth century. The structure covers three crypts. The basic exterior is Gothic, and much of the abbey is Romanesque.

The interior includes a stairway with 43,000 steps; a magnificent cloister with statues, and a large dining hall with intriguing narrow windows. From the medieval walls surrounding the abbey, the panoramic view of St. Malo Bay is beautiful.

The interior of the abbey is unique, but from a distance, the magnitude, intricacy, and grandeur of the mountain, and its abbey, would attract the angels.

The Abbey at Nesle La Reposte

Nine kilometers north of Villenauxe, the remarkable ruins of an abbey built by Clovis (king of the Franks) in the sixth century are hidden from view on a narrow country road. According to conventional wisdom, the wife of Clovis suggested that if he won a major military victory, he should build the abbey. He must have been victorious.

During the Middle Ages, the abbey was designated "Royal," which conveyed special church significance. At the acme of its greatness, there were four thousand people residing in the contemporary small village at Nesle. The name is probably derived from "nest." At one time, two thousand monks resided at the abbey.

Today, the ruins, which are part of the grounds of a private home, are impressive and inspiring, but the religious purpose that motivated the construction is no longer in evidence.

The Church at Villenauxe

In 1212, the Church of St. Pierre–St. Paul was built at Villenauxe by the Augustinians. In 1224, the first clock was installed. In 1499, the church acquired its present name. In 1567, it was sacked by the French Protestant Huguenots, who, at the same time, sacked the abbey at Nesle, then controlled by the Benedictines.

In 1832, the Church of St. Pierre–St. Paul was the storm center for a cholera epidemic that virtually decimated the population of the city. In 1840, the church was declared a national monument. On June 13, 1940, it was destroyed again by a German air raid. In 1945, the church was partially renovated, and in February 1992, a twelve-year major reconstruction was launched.

If a church in the United States had survived for eight centuries, imagine the impact on the parishioners and the community. On the other hand, if such a church existed in the United States, the tribal dancing around a central bonfire would remind us of its heritage.

Sens

The Cathedral of Saint Etienne at Sens was begun in A.D. 1130 with some of the chapels not being completed until the seventeenth century. It is considered an outstanding Gothic cathedral.

The main exterior façade is composed of three portals and two towers. The interior, as with most European cathedrals, is somber and unengaging; however, the premises ooze with history.

The mausoleum of the Dauphin, the son of Louis XV, and a magnificent series of stained glass windows, installed in the twelfth century, are featured. Four of the windows depict scenes from the life of St. Thomas Becket.

The treasury of the Sens cathedral is one of the richest in France. The loot is highlighted by a unique collection of Coptic and Persian fabrics, liturgical vestments and shrouds, and ivory objects pilfered from the most remote locations on Earth.

Fontenay Abbey

Because of our special interest in Cistercian architecture, we visited the twelfth-century monastery at Fontenay in Burgundy.

At the abbey, during its prime, more than three hundred monks practiced their faith. That level of effort was sustained for more than four centuries. During the French Revolution, the abbey was converted to a paper mill. At the beginning of the twentieth century, private owners restored the original buildings.

Simplicity is the essence of Cistercian architecture. The austere, uncluttered style insures welcome relief from the typical Christian structure. The basic Cistercian style was copied precisely at every abbey representing this order. St. Bernard, of Swiss hostel fame, created the Cistercian Order in Burgundy, and Fontenay was his personal preference.

The main church is relatively small; however, the absence of clutter creates a grandeur that transcends the building's dimensions. The oak roof of the overhead dormitory, where the monks slept on straw, is next to a gigantic workroom overlooking the beautiful cloister. The Spartan nature of the Cistercian monkhood is illustrated by a fireplace in the kitchen, a small "warming room," and the absence of guest facilities. There was no source of heat in the church, the dormitory, and the workroom.

The forge, infirmary, prison, kennels, gardens (including herbs), dovecote, and extensive outbuildings represent the ultimate of simplicity and remarkable independence from the world outside.

A Cistercian monk led a difficult life. It is clear that devotion, rather than posturing, was the sustaining religious rationale.

THE COLOGNE CATHEDRAL

As with most major German cities, Cologne was virtually destroyed by Allied bombing in World War II; however, the shell of the medieval Gothic cathedral survived, and the exterior has been rebuilt with tender loving care.

The cathedral ("Dom" in German) was constructed in the thirteenth century, and it is one of the largest and most impressive in the world. The twin 515-foot towers are overpowering, and the external façades, although generously ornate, dominate the landscape from every direction. The interior is dark and uninviting, but the historic objet d'art, the bejeweled shrine of the Three Holy Kings, the stained glass windows, and the elaborately carved stalls for the members of the choir illustrate the wealth and power of the Catholic Church and the predominant role of Catholicism in western European history.

THE KESTREL'S EYE

The Kestrel's Eye is an extraordinary movie. Filmed in Malmo, Sweden, it chronicles one year in the life of a pair of kestrels (a raptor in the Falcon family). They maintain a nest in the belfry of a thirteenth-century church. Three years were required for filming, but only the cycle of a single year is depicted on film.

Michael Kristersson directed the production, and there is no narration. From the perspective of the kestrel's eye, humanity is observed particularly as it pertains to the activities of the church. The kestrel pair watch the tender care of the cemetery in front of the church: a wedding, a funeral, and the shoveling of snow. Actual sounds are omnipresent including the lowing of cows in an adjoining field, automobiles, the voices of the congregation, and the chatter of blackbirds, starlings, and house martins, all of which share the church premises.

The camera joins the male kestrel on hunting expeditions, and the bird's-eye view of life is mesmerizing. Four cameras capture the travail, commitment, and comedy associated with the maturation of six young kestrels from the egg to initial flight. The human species also reflects a comical dimension through the eyes of a kestrel.

The Kestrel's Eye deserves a distinguished international documentary award. Through the medium of a unique motion picture, a church comes alive.

St. James's in London

After a few hours sleep, and a delicious British-style breakfast, we walked to Buckingham Palace to see the "Trooping of the Colors" on the queen's birthday. Because of the dense crowds, we returned via a detour that included Piccadilly Circus, the arts and crafts market, and St. James's Church.

The church architect was Sir Christopher Wren, and the church was consecrated in 1684. The first rector became the archbishop of Canterbury. The congregation represents a progression of celebrities.

In 1940, the church was virtually destroyed by German bombs. The restoration was completed in 1954. The garden includes a catalpa tree from the state of Georgia that was transplanted by James Oglethorpe (the founder of the state). A number of artists from the Royal Academy are interred on the premises.

If the Christian church did not exist, the history of the West would lack color and continuity.

A Hungarian Basilica

At the bend of the Danube River, about thirty-five miles northwest of Budapest, we drove along the river and observed the ruins of the four-teenth-century Arpad Royal Castle, which was built by Bela IV. At Esztergom, we visited the basilica that serves as the center of the Roman Catholic Church in Hungary. The small basilica is constructed of Italian carrara marble. It served as a retreat for Pope John Paul II in 1991.

In the crypt, the tomb of Archbishop Mindszenty is prominently displayed. As cardinal, Mindszenty opposed both Fascism and Commu-nism in Hungary. In 1949, he was convicted of treason by the Commu-nist regime for his failure to secularize the Catholic schools. He was sen-tenced to life imprisonment.

During the 1956 Hungarian Revolution, Cardinal Mindszenty was freed. Before he could be recaptured, he found asylum at the United States Embassy in Budapest, where he was under house arrest for twelve years.

Cardinal Mindszenty served as a symbol of freedom for all of eastern Europe. It is incongruous that freedom, in that context, is equated with the perpetuation of Roman Catholic control of the school system.

SAN FRANCISCO IN CARACAS

At the Iglesia de San Francisco in Caracas, Venezuela, where we observed a noon mass, we were again confronted with the correlation between the Roman Catholic Church and history. San Francisco was the situs where Simon Bolivar was proclaimed "El Libertador" in 1813 and where his funeral was conducted in 1842.

At the Palacio Municipal, where the city council of Caracas meets, three presidents of Venezuela were inaugurated in a small chapel that fronts on the atrium. The lovely atrium, with tropical plantings, featured a remarkable life-sized creche that occupied half of the area of the atrium.

The separation of church and state is a doctrine that receives slight notice outside of the geographical confines of the United States and Great Britain.

CHURCH ARCHITECTURE IN THE UNITED STATES

At the beginning of the nineteenth century, the political and social leadership of New York City attended the Grace Church at East 11th Street and Broadway in Manhattan. In recent years, racial and ethnic realities have intervened, but the Grace Church still represents an architectural jewel.

The church is small, attractive, and inviting, and still mirrors the special care of an affluent congregation. The stained glass windows are vintage Tiffany. Although many contemporary lamps are superior, sunlight through Tiffany glass still constitutes a special treat.

After exploring English cathedrals and the Catholic cathedral genre in Europe, it is difficult to wax philosophical about the relatively recent American church architecture (unless you reside in a small town in Vermont). American churches lack the historic context, the construction expertise, and the unlimited time that allowed the great European cathedrals to flourish.

The purpose of this church architectural litany, in a tract about religion, illustrates the domination of the cathedral as the political and social situs of major historical developments in western Europe. The history of western Europe and the history of the major cathedrals were intimately related. The cathedral was utilized as a community center, and important events that transcended religious doctrine were staged in the church.

The architecture of the European church personifies religious dogma, but the events that transpire in the church are significantly laic.

SCULPTURE AND ART

From the sixth century B.C., Buddhism and Hinduism portrayed gods and other religious icons in sculptured manifestations. In the fourth century B.C., divinities and effigies were common subjects of sculpture. During the reign of Alexander the Great, Lysippus, who directed the School of Argos and Sicyon, completed hundreds of works in bronze, including a statue of Zeus that has survived on bronze coins. Both Buddhist and Greek sculptors used the idealized human form to portray God. Although the definition of "religion" presents formidable obstacles, most scholars concur that relevant religious experience was depicted in sculpture before the birth of Christ.

In the Borghese Museum in Rome, the collection of Roman art features copies of Greek sculpture from the Hellenistic Period (first century A.D.). Muses and gods are represented along with athletes, soldiers, and statesmen. The results are natural, diverse, and esthetically rewarding.

In contrast, the Christian works, with the delightful exception of Giovanni Bernini, are stereotyped, simplistic, unnatural, stylized, and devoid of appeal. In Bernini's *Abduction of Proserpina*, the detail appears to come alive. The marble fingers of the abductor make lifelike imprints in the flesh of the leg and rib cage of Proserpina, and the bronze figure of Neptune is electrifying.

It is remarkable that an unprovable belief in fables pertaining to a Christian version of God could present centuries of tasteless, dogmatic sameness in sculpture featuring the inevitable angels, madonnas, and resurrections. Even the concept of resurrection was described occasionally in literary and artistic form by Greek and Roman writers and artists centuries before the birth of Christ.

All forms of art must be nurtured by the environment in which the artist lives and works. That controlling factor accounts for the historic Western preoccupation with Christianity in art. For many centuries, the external stimulation was confined to angels and icons. Today, the references to angels are confined to a few sermons, Christmas decorations, and an infrequent reference in the courting game. Most of the other icons, from many cultures, have survived modernity and have been perpetuated in religious works.

RELIGIOUS VIEWS
OF DISSIDENTS
(and Others)

Stringfellow Barr (citing an Arab saying): "Better one act of justice than seven years of prayer."

Robert Browning: "Ah, but a man's reach should exceed his grasp or what's a heaven for?"

Fred I. Cairns: "He who works for a better world is as likely to achieve satisfactory results as is he who but prays for it."

G. K. Chesterton: "The religion of the future will be based, to a considerable extent, on a more highly developed and differentiated, subtle form of humor."

Tristran Coffin: "The church has learned that truth is unpalatable to most men, and so science poses no real peril to the pulpit."

Cyril Connolly: "Yet, I know that there are thousands like me: . . . pagans who still live by Christian morals."

Mary B. G. Eddy: "God is Good."

J. G. Frazer: "Religion consists of two elements, a theoretical and a

147

practical, namely, a belief in powers higher than man and an attempt to propitiate or please them."

Thomas Huxley: "How silly of me not to have thought of that" (upon reading Darwin's *On the Origin of Species*).

William J. Lederer and Eugene Burdick: "Finian learned that the faith of a communist was no more shaken by news of a bloody purge of 'right-wing deviationists' than is the faith of a Catholic by the news that the Inquisition was brutal."

Konrad Lorenz: "If I thought of man as the final image of God, I should not know what to think of God."

Bertrand Russell: "You are an atheist. What will you say if you meet Him in Heaven? 'God, you gave us insufficient evidence.'"

George Bernard Shaw: "The text of (the Golden Rule) should not be taken quite literally for though a man might like his uncle to die and leave him a million he could hardly set the example."

Vincent Sheean: "The more churches there are, the less there is of religion."

Francis C. M. Wei: "If a person neglects what man can do and seeks for what Heaven does, he fails to understand the nature of things."

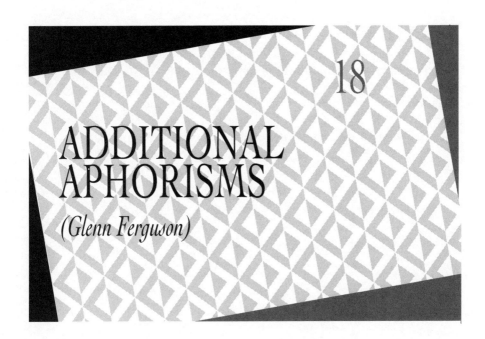

ADDITIONAL APHORISMS
(Glenn Ferguson)

The meaning of life is life.

Live life with distinction, and death will lose its fear.

Faith cannot counterbalance the randomness of risk.

Everlasting punishment does not represent Christian charity.

When religion becomes conviction, acumen disappears.*

A religious dogma is as true as or as false as its competitors.

Each religious sect reflects a modicum of truth.

Religious credo should be treated as a virus.

Practicing charity is preferable to preaching it.

Blasphemy was devised and nurtured by bigots.

For Jesus, the Day of Judgment was imminent; therefore, proof was not his preoccupation.

Religious beliefs are based on the tenet that righteousness flows from comprehension of the incomprehensible.

Investigative reporting does not explore religion.

Passion, not conviction, motivates religious activism.

Homo sapiens needs a paradigm on Earth rather than in Heaven.

CONCLUSION

*When we are unable
to comprehend,
God is the mind's defense.*

Based on longevity and study, I am increasingly reluctant to accept the credo of any religious faith or sect. As human beings, we have conceived of God in our own image. As doctrine is interpreted, the dogma of any separate sect becomes narrower and more differentiated. These sectarian schisms are not merely the nuances that distinguish a Unitarian from a Methodist and that originate from a common base.

The variations are fundamentally cultural. Many religious faiths have been created without knowledge of the proximity of others. These faiths were not severed from a paradigm but were "cut from whole cloth." The substantive difference is not the ritual of baptism but the interpretation of the nature of God and of life on Earth, and in the hereafter, which are dictated by that interpretation.

On a comparative basis, the Buddhist concept of Nirvana may become more meaningful than the Christian Heaven. The Taoist concept of family may become more satisfying than the Hindu. The Roman Catholic or Episcopal ritual may become more reassuring than the loose structure of a fundamentalist sect.

151

Modern eclectic thinking tends to create the ambience in which a new denomination or credo, Heaven forbid, may be nurtured. I choose to ignore that temptation and to request greater clarity, and honesty, among the existing flocks.